MICROSOFT

AZURE

A Complete Guide for Beginners

Microsoft Azure Tutorial

Windows Azure, which was later renamed as Microsoft Azure in 2014, is a cloud computing platform, designed by Microsoft to successfully build, deploy, and manage applications and services through a global network of datacenters. This tutorial explains various features of this flexible platform and provides a step-by-step description of how to use the same.

Audience

This tutorial has been designed for software developers who are keen on developing best-in-class applications using this open and advanced platform of Windows Azure.

Prerequisites

To learn Windows Azure, you need to be familiar with the Windows environment and have a basic knowledge of cloud computing.

© 2017 COPYRIGHT

DISCLAIMERS

Table of Contents

Cloud Computing – Overview 14

Architecture of Cloud Computing 16

Types of Cloud...17

Benefits of Cloud 19

SPI 20

Microsoft Azure - Windows 21

Azure as PaaS (Platform as a Service) 22

Azure as IaaS (Infrastructure as a Service)..24

Azure Management Portal...27

Microsoft Azure - Components 29

Compute / Execution Models...30

Data Management 31

Networking...32

Big Data and Big Compute 34

Messaging 35

sCaching...36

Identity and Access 37

Mobile Service..38

Backup 39

Media...40

Commerce...40

Software Development Kit (SDK) 41

Microsoft Azure - Compute Module 42

Create a Web App 43

Create a Virtual Machine 46

Creating a Mobile Service...51

Creating Batch Service..52

Microsoft Azure - Fabric Controller 54

Microsoft Azure - Storage 57

Creating Azure Storage Account...57

Storage Account Endpoints..61

Generating an Access Key 62

Managing Data to Azure Storage 63

Microsoft Azure - Blobs..65

Create a Container 66

Upload a Blob using PowerShell...67

Download a Blob 69

Manage Blobs using Azure Storage Explorer 70

Microsoft Azure - Queues 71

Considerations...73

Managing Queues using PowerShell 74

Managing Queues using Azure Storage Explorer......................78

Microsoft Azure - Tables..80

How to Manage Tables Using PowerShell...................................81

How to Manage Table using Azure Storage Explorer 88

Microsoft Azure - CDN 92

Create a CDN 93

Create CDN for Custom Origin Links..95

Manage CDN...96

Map a Custom Domain Name...100

Microsoft Azure - Applications 102

Microsoft Azure - Security..104

Creating an Active Directory...105

Mapping a Custom Domain...108

Creating Users...110

Integrating with Azure Active Directory 113

Integrating On-Premise Active Directory...115

Reports..116

Microsoft Azure - Datacenters 117

How to Choose the Right Data Center for Your Application 119

Microsoft Azure - Scenarios...120

Software Development..121

Enterprise Process Offloading 122

Enterprise Application Integration 123

Microsoft Azure - Management Portal 124

Create a New Application 126

Check Credit and Subscriptions 127

Add a New Subscription...130

Azure Preview Portal 132

Microsoft Azure - Create Virtual Network..134

Creating a Virtual Network in Clouds Only...134

Creating a Virtual Network in Cloud Only (Advanced Settings)...........................136

Microsoft Azure - Deploying Virtual Machines..139

Quick Create 140

Create Virtual Machine with Advanced Settings 142

Connecting with a Virtual Network 146

Accessing the Virtual Machine 147

Considerations 147

Microsoft Azure - Endpoint Configuration....................................148

Access Control of Endpoint 152

Microsoft Azure - Point-to-Site Connectivity 154

Enabling Point-to-Site Connectivity on Existing Virtual Network.......155

Create a New Virtual Network with Point-to-site Connectivity 157

Generate Certificates 162

Microsoft Azure - Site-to-Site Connectivity..................................170

Creating a Site-to-Site Connectivity Network...............................171

Microsoft Azure - Traffic Manager..176

Create Traffic Manager...177

Create Endpoints to be Monitored via Traffic Manager 179

Configure the Policy 181

Microsoft Azure - PowerShell...183

Installing Azure PowerShell 184

Connecting to Your Subscription..186

Connect to Your Azure Account 188

Remove Azure Account...191

Get Help 192

Microsoft Azure - Monitoring Virtual Machines............................193

Monitor VM in Azure Management Portal. 194

Enable Diagnostics...199

Microsoft Azure - Setting Up Alert Rules 201

Microsoft Azure - Application Deployment 204

Deploying a Web App from PowerShell...205

Create a Deployment Package..206

Create a Website in Azure using PowerShell...208

Deploy Website using Deployment Package 209

Microsoft Azure - Backup & Recovery 210

Create Backup Vault...211

Schedule a Backup...214

Microsoft Azure - Self-Service Capabilities...217

Group Management..217

Password Management 217

Microsoft Azure - Multi-Factor Authentication....................................219

Create a Multi-Factor Authentication Provider 221

Enable the Multi-Factor Authentication for Existing Directory................223

Enable Multi-Factor Authentication for On-premises Applications...........224

Microsoft Azure - Forefront Identity Manager.....................................226

Microsoft Azure - Data Import & Export Job 229

Data Export Job 229

Create an Export Job 229

Create Import job 233

Microsoft Azure - Websites...234

Create a Website in Azure Management Portal.....................................235

Deploying Azure Website from Visual Studio 236

Monitoring the Website...239

Staged Publishing..241

Add a Deployment Slot for Testing Before Production...........................241

Microsoft Azure - Scalability...242

Microsoft Azure - Disk Configuration..248

Virtual Machine and Disks...249

Create/Attach a Disk in Virtual Machine 250

Configure the Disk in Virtual Machine 252

Delete the Disk 254

Image Disks 255

Microsoft Azure - Disk Caching 259

Microsoft Azure - Personalize Access 261

Azure - Personalize Company Branding 267

Active Free Trial of Azure Active Directory (ADD) Premium Edition 268

Customize Branding 269

Login with Customized Sign-in Page 273

Azure - Self-Service Password Reset 274

Azure - Self-Service Group Management 278

Policy Setup for Self-service Group Management 279

Microsoft Azure - Create a Group 281

Microsoft Azure - Security Reports & Alerts 283

Anomalies Reports 283

Activity Reports 284

Integrated Application 286

Search Activity of a Particular User 287

Azure Active Directory Editions and Reports 288

Microsoft Azure - Orchestrated Recovery 289

Create a Site Recovery Vault 290

Between On-premises VMM Site and Azure 291

Between On-premises Hyper-V Site and Azure 293

Between On-premises Site with VMWare / Physical Server and Azure 294

Between Two On-premises VMWare Sites 296

Between Two On-premises VMM Sites and SAN Array Application 297

Prerequisites 298

Create a Recovery Plan 299

Microsoft Azure - Health Monitoring..300

Microsoft Azure - Upgrades..302

Update a Cloud Service 303

VIP (Virtual IP) Swap..305

Considerations 306

Cloud Computing – Overview

The popular trend in today's technology driven world is 'Cloud Computing'. Cloud computing can be referred to as the storing and accessing of data over the internet rather than your computer's hard drive. This means you don't access the data from either your computer's hard drive or over a dedicated computer network (home or office network). Cloud computing means data is stored at a remote place and is synchronized with other web information.

One prominent example of cloud computing is Office 365 which allows users to store, access, edit their MS Office documents online (in browser) without installing the actual program on their device.

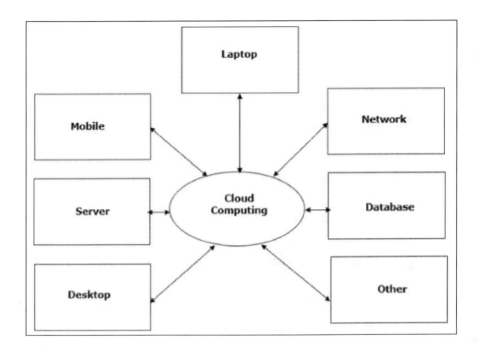

Architecture of Cloud Computing

The architecture of cloud computing comprises of the following components –

- Front-end device
- Back-end platform
- Cloud-based delivery
- Network

Front-end Devices – These are basically the devices that are used by clients to access the data or program using the browser or special applications.

Back-end Platform – There are various computers, servers, virtual machines, etc. that combine to become a back-end platform.

Types of Cloud

The storage options on cloud is in 3 forms –

- Public

- Private

- Hybrid

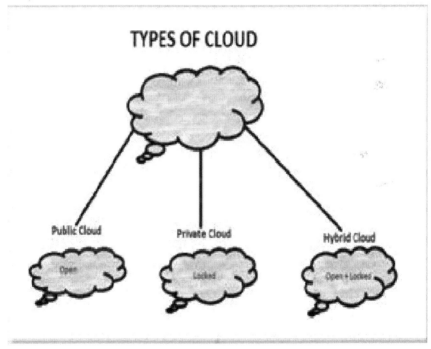

Public Cloud – A service provider makes the clouds available to the general public which is termed as a public cloud. These clouds are accessed through internet by users. These are open to public and their infrastructure is owned and operated by service providers as in case of Google and Microsoft.

Private Cloud – These clouds are dedicated to a particular organization. That particular organization can use the cloud for storing the company's data, hosting business application, etc. The data stored on private cloud can't be shared with other organizations. The cloud is managed either by the organization itself or by the third party.

Hybrid Cloud – When two or more clouds are bound together to offer the advantage of both public and private clouds, they are termed as Hybrid Cloud. Organizations can use private clouds for sensitive application, while public clouds for non-sensitive applications. The hybrid clouds provide flexible, scalable and cost-effective solutions to the organizations.

Benefits of Cloud

There are many benefits of clouds. Some of them are listed below.

- Cloud service offers scalability. Allocation and de-allocation of resources is dynamically as per demand.

- It saves on cost by reducing capital infrastructure.

- It allows the user to access the application independent of their location and hardware configuration.

- It simplifies the network and lets the client access the application without buying license for individual machine.

- Storing data on clouds is more reliable as it is not lost easily.

SPI

Next comes how cloud services are categorized. S stand for Software, P stands for Platform and I for Infrastructure in SPI. SaaS is Software as a service; PaaS is Platform as a service and IaaS is Infrastructure as a Service.

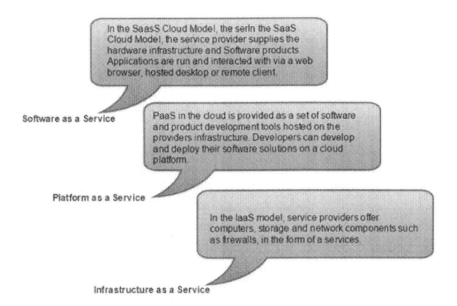

Following are the live examples of these models.

- **SAAS Model** – E-mail (Gmail, Yahoo, etc.)

- **PASS Model** – Microsoft Azure

- **IAAS Model** – Amazon S3

Microsoft Azure - Windows

There are many cloud computing platforms offered by different organizations. Windows Azure is one of them, which is provided by Microsoft. Azure can be described as the managed data centers that are used to build, deploy, manage the applications and provide services through a global network. The services provided by Microsoft Azure are PaaS and IaaS. Many programming languages and frameworks are supported by it.

Azure as PaaS (Platform as a Service)

As the name suggests, a platform is provided to clients to develop and deploy software. The clients can focus on the application development rather than having to worry about hardware and infrastructure. It also takes care of most of the operating systems, servers and networking issues.

Pros

- The overall cost is low as the resources are allocated on demand and servers are automatically updated.

- It is less vulnerable as servers are automatically updated and being checked for all known security issues. The whole process is not visible to developer and thus does not pose a risk of data breach.

- Since new versions of development tools are tested by the Azure team, it becomes easy for developers to move on to new tools. This also helps the developers to meet the customer's demand by quickly adapting to new versions.

Cons

- There are portability issues with using PaaS. There can be a different environment at Azure, thus the application might have to be adapted accordingly.

Azure as IaaS (Infrastructure as a Service)

It is a managed compute service that gives complete control of the operating systems and the application platform stack to the application developers. It lets the user to access, manage and monitor the data centers by themselves.

Pros

- This is ideal for the application where complete control is required. The virtual machine can be completely adapted to the requirements of the organization or business.

- IaaS facilitates very efficient design time portability. This means application can be migrated to Windows Azure without rework. All the application dependencies such as database can also be migrated to Azure.

- IaaS allows quick transition of services to clouds, which helps the vendors to offer services to their clients easily. This also helps the vendors to expand their business by selling the existing software or services in new markets.

Cons

- Since users are given complete control they are tempted to stick to a particular version for the dependencies of applications. It might become difficult for them to migrate the application to future versions.

- There are many factors which increases the cost of its operation. For example, higher server maintenance for patching and upgrading software.

- There are lots of security risks from unpatched servers. Some companies have welldefined processes for testing and updating on-premise servers for security vulnerabilities. These processes need to be extended to the cloud-hosted IaaS VMs to mitigate hacking risks.

- The unpatched servers pose a great security risk. Unlike PaaS, there is no provision of automatic server patching in IaaS. An unpatched server with sensitive information can be very vulnerable affecting the entire business of an organization.

- It is difficult to maintain legacy apps in Iaas. It can be stuck with the older version of the operating systems and application stacks. Thus, resulting in applications that are difficult to maintain and add new functionality over the period of time.

It becomes necessary to understand the pros and cons of both services in order to choose the right one according your requirements. In conclusion it can be said that, PaaS has definite economic advantages for operations over IaaS for commodity applications. In PaaS, the cost of operations breaks the business model. Whereas, IaaS gives complete control of the OS and application platform stack.

Azure Management Portal

Azure Management Portal is an interface to manage the services and infrastructure launched in 2012. All the services and applications are displayed in it and it lets the user manage them.

Getting started

A free trial account can be created on Azure management portal by visiting the following link - manage.windowsazure.com

The screen that pops up is as shown in the following image. The account can be created using our existing Gmail, Hotmail or Yahoo account.

Once logged in, you will be redirected to the following screen, where there is a list of services and applications on the left panel.

When you click on a category, its details are displayed on the screen. You can see the number of applications, virtual machine, mobile services and so on by clicking on the menu item.

The next chapter contains a detailed explanation of how to use this portal to manage Azure services.

Microsoft Azure - Components

Categorizing the services would help you understand Azure better. These categories are termed as 'Components' in this tutorial. The Individual components are explained with detailed pictures in subsequent chapters.

Compute / Execution Models

This is the interface for executing the application, which is one of the basic functions of Azure.

As seen in the above image, there are different models such as Web App, Virtual Machine, Mobile Service, Cloud Service, and Batch Service. These models can be used either separately or in combination as per the requirement.

Data Management

Data management can be done by using SQL server Database component or the simple data storage module offered by Windows Azure. SQL server database can be used for relational database. The storage module can store unrelated tables (without foreign key or any relation) and blobs. Blobs include binary data in the form of images, audio, video, and text files.

Networking

Azure traffic manager routes the requests of a user intelligently to an available datacenter. The process involves finding the nearest datacenter to the user who makes the request for web application, and if the nearest datacenter is not available due to various reasons, the traffic manager deviates the request to another datacenter. However, rules are set by the owner of the application as to how a traffic manager should behave.

The virtual network is another feature that is part of networking in services offered by Windows Azure. The virtual network allows a network between local machines at your premise and virtual machine in Azure Datacenter. IPs to virtual machines can be assigned in a way that makes them appear to be residing in your own premise. The virtual network is set up using a Virtual Private Network (VPN) device.

The following image shows how these two features actually look in Azure portal.

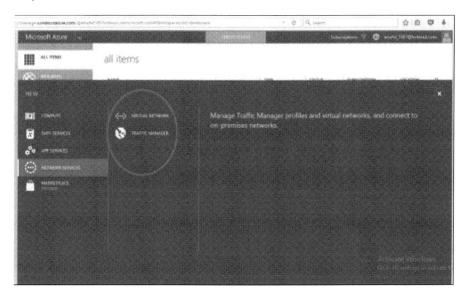

Big Data and Big Compute

The large amount of data can be stored and managed using Windows Azure. Azure offers HDInsight which is Hadoop-based service. Organizations often need to manage large amount of data which is necessarily not relational database management. Hadoop is a prominent technology used these days. Thus, Azure offers Hadoop service on their platform for clients.

The term 'Big Compute' refers to high performing computations. This is achieved by executing code on many machines at the same time.

Messaging

Windows Azure offers two options for handling the interactions between two apps. One falls under storage component of the service and is called **'Message Queues'**. The other one comes under the app service and is called **'Service Bus'**. The messages can be sent to initiate communication among different components of an application or among different applications using these two options.

Caching

Microsoft Azure offers two kinds of caching which are in-memory Caching and Content Delivery Network (CDN) for caching frequently accessed data and improves the application performance. CDN is used to cache the blob data that will be accessed faster by users around the world.

Identity and Access

This component is about management of users, authentication and authorization. Active directory stores the information of users accessing the application and also the organization's information. It can synchronize with the related information on local machines residing on premises. Multifactor Access (MFA) service is built to address the security concerns such as only the right user can access the application.

Mobile Service

Windows Azure offers a very easy platform to develop mobile application. You can simply start using mobile development tools after logging into your account. You don't have to write big custom codes for the mobile application if you use this service. The push notifications can be sent, data can be stored and users can be authenticated in very less time.

Backup

The site recovery service replicates the data at secondary location as well as automates the process of recovery of data in case of data outage. Similarly Azure backup can be used to backing up the on premise data in clouds. Data is stored in encrypted mode in both the cases. Windows Azure offers a very effective and reliable backup service to clients and ensures they don't face inconvenience in case of hardware failures.

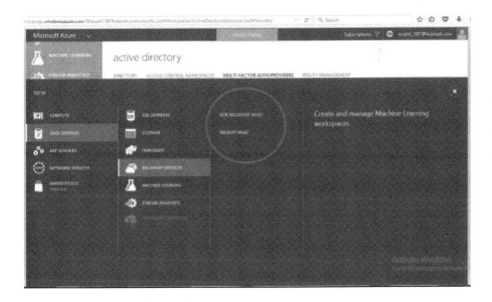

Media

This service addresses multiple concerns related to uploading media and making it available to end users easily. Users can manage tasks related to the media like encoding, ad insertion, streaming, etc. easily.

Commerce

Windows Azure offers the opportunity to users to buy or sell applications and data through their platform. The applications are put in the marketplace or Azure store from where they can be accessed and bought by other users.

Software Development Kit (SDK)

Azure applications can be produced by the developers in various programming languages. Microsoft currently provides language-specific SDKs for Java, .NET, PHP, Node.js, Ruby, and Python. There is also a general Windows Azure SDK that supports language, such as C++.

Microsoft Azure - Compute Module

In the last chapter, we explained how to create an Azure account. In this chapter, you will find step by step explanation of each component –

Step 1 – First, login in to your Azure account.

Step 2 – Click 'New' at the left bottom corner and drag your cursor to 'Compute'.

Now you will see a list of models under Compute Model as shown in the following image.

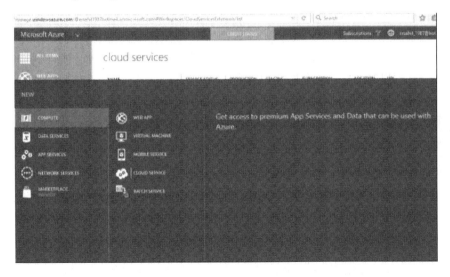

Create a Web App

Step 1 – Click Web App.

Step 2 – Click Quick Create and enter the URL and choose a service plan from the dropdown list as shown in the following image.

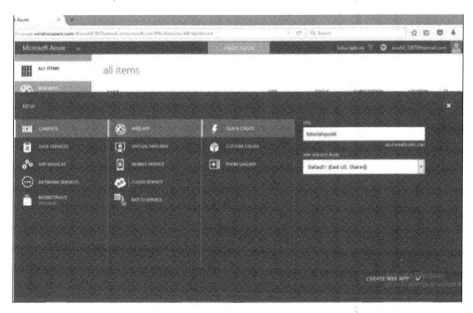

When you go back to the main screen, it will show the website just created. And when you click the website URL, it will take you to the website.

e

The following image shows how your website will look when you click the URL.

Similarly, you can choose 'From Gallery' when creating a web app instead of 'Quick Create'. This will let you choose the development framework in which you want to create your app.

Windows Azure supports .Net, Java, PHP, Python, Node.js and Ruby. There are several ways of publishing the code to Azure server. It can be published using FTP, FTPs, Microsoft Web Deploy technology. Various source control tools such as GitHub, Dropbox and Codeplex can also be used to publish the code. It provides a very interactive interface to keep track of changes that have been published already and also unpublished changes.

Create a Virtual Machine

Step 1 – Click on 'Virtual Machine' from the list.

Step 2 – Then click 'From Gallery'.

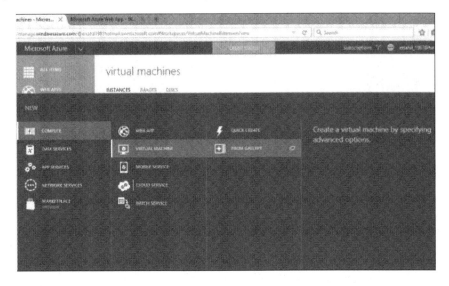

Step 3 – Choose the Operating System or Program you want to run.

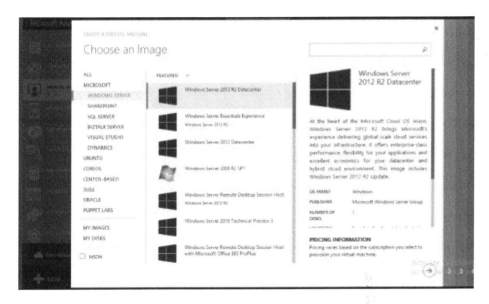

Step 4 – Choose the configuration and fill in the details.

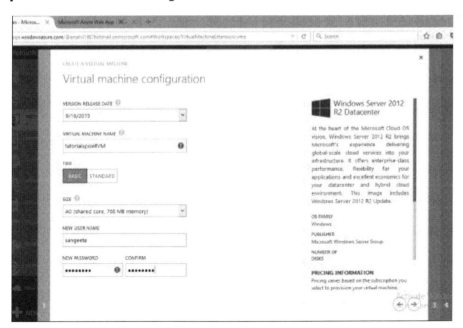

The Username and Password you set up here will be needed to access the virtual machine every time.

On the next two screens you can leave the default values on for the first time.

Step 5 – The virtual machine just created will be displayed when you click on 'Virtual Machine' on the left panel as shown in following image. It might take a few minutes to show up.

Step 6 – Once the machine is created you can connect to it by clicking on the connect icon displayed at the bottom of the screen. It will save a .rpd file on your machine as shown in the following image. Chose 'save file' on the screen and it will save in 'downloads' or the in the set location on your machine.

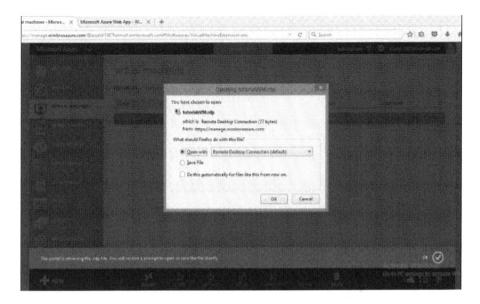

Step 7 – Open that .rpd file and you can connect to the VM by filling in the credentials into the following screen.

You can also use your own image by capturing the image of an existing virtual machine or virtual hard drive. Virtual machines are beneficial in several ways.

- A user can try new operating system without actually installing them.

- A VM can be deleted when you are done with the operating system.

- New versions of an operating system can be tried and tested before the user installs them on the machine.

- VM provides a very economical and hassle free way of using a development framework or a tool that runs on specific version of OS.

Creating a Mobile Service

Mobile services compute hosting model is optimized to provide a cloud backend for applications that run on mobile devices. For creating a mobile service –

Step 1 – Select Mobile services under Compute and click on create. A new window will be open as shown in the following image.

Step 2 – Fill in the URL. Select the database, region and backend.

Step 3 – Tick the check box if you want to configure the advance push settings. This option allows us to configure our Mobile Service to use an existing notification hub or specify the name of a new one. If you leave this checkbox unmarked, a new hub will be created in a new namespace with a default name.

Creating Batch Service

Batch service is needed when a large scale application is run and a parallel high performing computing is required. The developers can create batches to run a task parallel that eases the workload at no extra cost. Azure charges for only the virtual machines which are being used. They can schedule a task, put them in queues and manage the workload in cloud. Batch creation does not involve setting up a separate VM, cluster or job scheduling.

To creating a batch service follow the similar steps for creating other services under Compute model. The following image shows how a batch service can be created quickly.

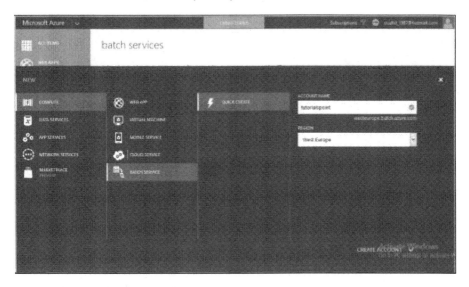

Once you have created a batch service, you can see the details by selecting it from the left panel. The following image pops up on the screen.

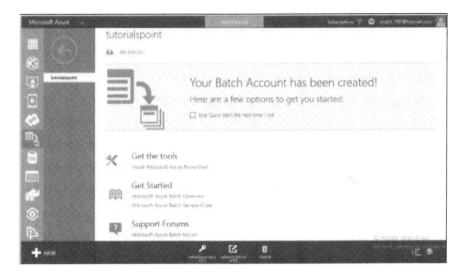

Microsoft Azure - Fabric Controller

Fabric Controller is a significant part of Windows Azure architecture. When thinking of the components or services provided by Windows Azure, we wonder how all this works and what is happening in clouds. It seems very complex from our end. Let us look into the physical architecture of these services to have a better understanding of Fabric Controller.

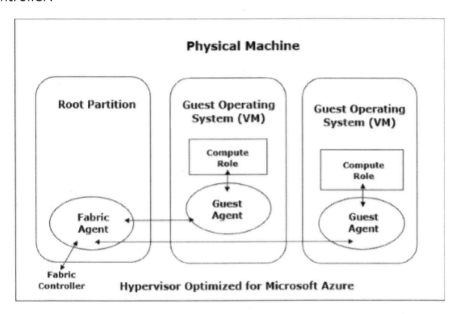

Inside the datacenter, there are many machines or servers aggregated by a switch. We can say that fabric controller is a brain of the azure service that analyses the processes and makes decisions. **Fabrics** are group of machines in Microsoft's datacenter which are aggregated by a switch. The group of these machines is called **cluster**. Each cluster is managed and owned by a fabric controller.

They are replicated along with these machines. It manages everything inside those machines, for e.g., load balancers, switches, etc. Each machine has a fabric agent running inside it and fabric controller can communicate with each fabric agent.

When selecting a virtual machine offered by Windows Azure services, there are five options to choose from. The configuration is as follows –

	Memory	CPU	Instance Storage
Extra Small	768 MB	Single core 1.0 GHz	20 GB
Small	1.75 GB	Single core 1.6 GHz	225 GB
Medium	3.5 GB	Dual core 1.6 GHz	490 GB
Large	7 GB	Four core 1.6 GHz	1,000 GB
Extra Large	14 GB	Eight core 1.6 GHz	2,040 GB

When a user chooses one of the virtual machine, the operating system, patch updates and software updates are performed by fabric controller. It decides where the new application should run which is one of the most important functions of Fabric Controller. It also selects the physical server to optimize hardware utilization.

When a new application is published in Azure, an application configuration file written in XML is also attached. The fabric controller reads those files in Microsoft datacenter and makes the setting accordingly.

In addition to managing the allocation of resources to a specific application, it also monitors the health of compute and storage services. It also makes the failure recoveries for a system.

Imagine a situation where four instances of web role are running, and one of them dies. The fabric controller will initiate a new instance to replace the dead one immediately. Similarly, in case any virtual machine fails, a new one is assigned by the fabric controller. It also resets the load balancers after assigning the new machine, so that it points to the new machine instantaneously. Thus, all the intelligent tasks are performed by the Fabric Controller in Windows Azure architecture.

Microsoft Azure - Storage

The Storage component of Windows Azure represents a durable store in the cloud. Windows Azure allows developers to store tables, blobs, and message queues. The storage can be accessed through HTTP. You can also create our own client; although Windows Azure SDK provides a client library for accessing the Storage.

In this chapter, we will learn how to create a Windows Azure Storage account and use it for storing data.

Creating Azure Storage Account

Step 1 – When you login into your Azure account, you can find 'Storage' under 'Data Services'.

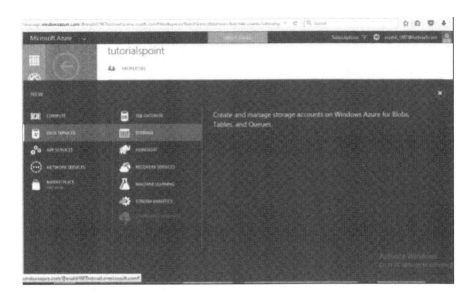

Step 2 – Click on 'Quick Create' and it will ask for 'Account Name'.

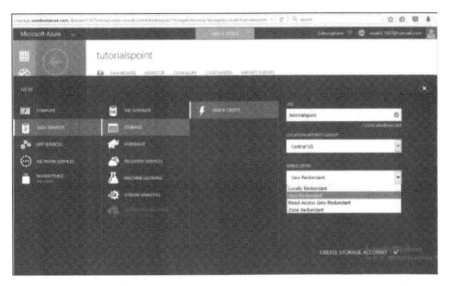

You can see there are four options in the 'Replication' dropdown. A copy of the data is kept so that it is durable and available at high speed. It is retained even in case of hardware failure. Let's see what these options mean –

- **Locally redundant storage** – Copy of the data is created in the same region where storage account is created. There are 3 copies of each request made against the data that resides on separate domains.

- **Zone-redundant storage (available for blobs only)** – Copy of the data is created on separate facilities either in the same region or across two regions. The advantage is that even if there is failure on one facility, the data still can be retained. Three copies of data are created. One more advantage is that data can be read from a secondary location.

- **Geo-redundant storage** – `Copy is created in a different region which means data is retained even if there is a failure in the complete region. The numbers of copies of data created are 6 in this case.

- **Read-access geo-redundant storage** – This option allows reading of data from a secondary location when data on the primary location is not available. The number of copies created is 6. The main advantage here is that availability of data can be maximized.

There are different price plans for each replication option and the 'Local Redundant' is the cheapest of them all. So, choosing the replication of data depends on the cost and individual requirements.

Storage Account Endpoints

Step 1 – Click on the 'Storage Account' it will take you to the next screen.

Step 2 – Click on 'Dashboard' from top horizontal menu.

Here you can see four items under services. You can create blobs, tables, queues and files in this storage account.

There will a unique URL for each object. For example, here account name is 'tutorialspoint' then the default URL for blob is **https://tutorialspoint.blob.core.windows.net** Similarly, replace blob with table, queue and file in the URL to get the respective URLs. To access an object in the location is appended in the URL. For example,

http://tutorialspoint.blob.core.windows.net/container1/blob1

Generating an Access Key

Access key is used to authenticate the access to the storage account. Two access keys are provided in order to access the account without interrupting it, in case, one key has to be regenerated.

To get the Access Keys, click on 'Manage Access Keys' in your storage account. The following screen will come up.

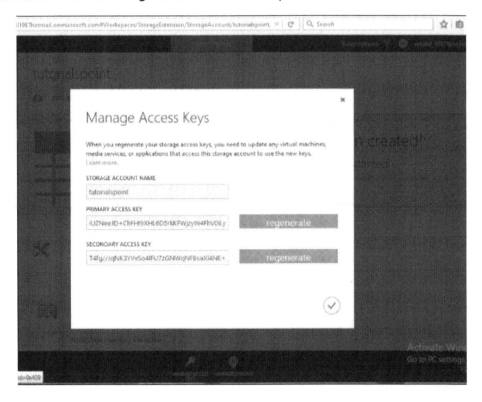

Regenerating the key at regular intervals is advised for security reasons.

Managing Data to Azure Storage

How can you upload or download data to Azure store? There are many ways to do it, but it can't be done within the Azure portal itself. You will have to either create your own application or use an already built tool.

There are many tools available for accessing the data in an explorer that can be accessed by clicking on 'Storage Explorer' under 'Get the Tools' in your Azure storage account. Alternatively, an application can also be built using Software Development Kit (SDK) available in Windows Azure Portal. Using the PowerShell commands is also an option to upload data. PowerShell is a command line application that facilitates administering and managing the Azure storage. Preset commands are used for different tasks to manage the storage.

You can install PowerShell by going to 'Downloads' on the following screen in your account. You will find it under Command-Line tools.

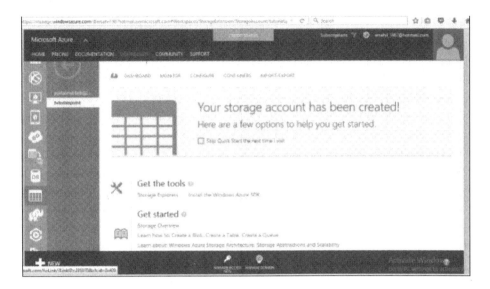

There are specific commands for each task. You can manage you storage account, create a new account, and create a container. Additionally, blobs, tables, queues messages can also be managed using PowerShell.

Microsoft Azure - Blobs

Let us first understand what a Blob is. The word 'Blob' expands to **B**inary **L**arge **OB**ject. Blobs include images, text files, videos and audios. There are three types of blobs in the service offered by Windows Azure namely block, append and page blobs.

- **Block blobs** are collection of individual blocks with unique block ID. The block blobs allow the users to upload large amount of data.

- **Append blobs** are optimized blocks that helps in making the operations efficient.

- **Page blobs** are compilation of pages. They allow random read and write operations. While creating a blob, if the type is not specified they are set to block type by default.

All the blobs must be inside a container in your storage. Here is how to create a container in Azure storage.

Create a Container

Step 1 – Go to Azure portal and then in your storage account.

Step 2 – Create a container by clicking 'Create new container' as shown in following image.

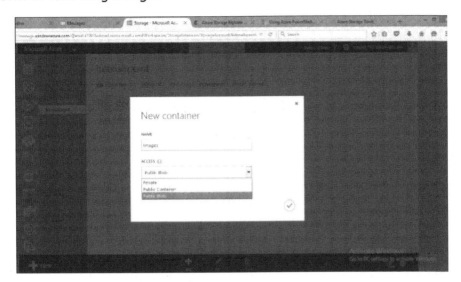

There are three options in the Access dropdown which sets the permission of who can access the blobs. 'Private' option will let only the account owner to access it. 'Public Container' will allow anonymous access to all the contents of that container. 'Public blob' option will set open access to blob but won't allow access to the container.

Upload a Blob using PowerShell

Step 1 – Go to 'Windows PowerShell' in the taskbar and right-click. Choose 'Run ISE as Administrator'.

Step 2 – Following command will let you access your account. You have to change the fields highlighted in all the commands.

```
$context = New-AzureStorageContext -StorageAccountName
    tutorialspoint StorageAccountKey

    iUZNeeJD+ChFHt9XHL6D5rkKFWjzyW4FhV0iLyvweDi+Xtzfy76juPzJ+mWt
    DmbqCWjsu/nr+1pqBJj rdOO2+A==
```

Step 3 – Run the following command. This will get you the details of you Azure account. This will make sure that your subscription is all set.

```
Get-AzureSubscription
```

Step 4 – Run the following command to upload your file.

```
Set-AzureStorageBlobContent -Blob Montiorlog.png -Container images -
    File
    "E:\MyPictures\MonitorLog.png" -Context $context -Force
```

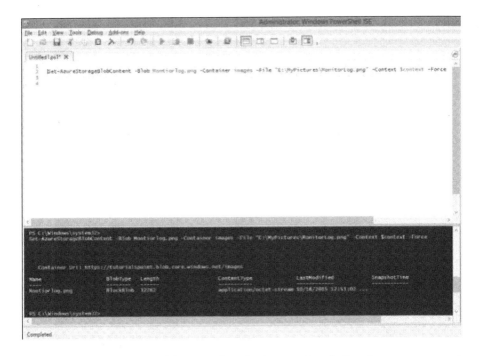

Step 5 – To check if the file is uploaded, run the following command.

```
Get-AzureStorageBlob -Container $ContainerName -Context $ctx | Select
    Name
```

Download a Blob

Step 1 – Set the directory where you want to download the file.

```
$localTargetDirectory = "C:\Users\Sahil\Downloads"
```

Step 2 – Download it.

```
$BlobName = "Montiorlog.png" Get-AzureStorageBlobContent -Blob
    $BlobName
    Container $ContainerName -Destination $localTargetDirectory
    -Context $ctx
```

Remember the following –

- All command names and file names are case sensitive.

- Commands should be in one line or should be continued in the next line by appending ` in the preceding line (` is continuation character in PowerShell)

Manage Blobs using Azure Storage Explorer

Managing blobs is pretty simple using 'Azure Storage Explorer' interface as it is just like Windows files and folder explorer. You can create a new container, upload blobs, see them in a listed format, and download them. Moreover, you can copy them to a secondary location in a very simple manner with this interface. The following image makes the process clear. As can be seen, once an account is added, we can select it from the dropdown and get going. It makes operating Azure storage very easy.

Microsoft Azure - Queues

In the common language used by developers, a queue is a data structure used to store data which follows First in-First out rule. A data item can be inserted from back of the queue while it is retrieved from front. Azure queues are a very similar concept that is used to store the messages in a queue. A sender sends the message and a client receives and processes them. A message has few attributes attached to it, for example expiry time.

A client usually processes and deletes the message. Windows Azure service lets the message to be stored for 7 days and later it gets deleted automatically, if it is not deleted by the client. There can be one sender and one client or one sender and many clients or many sender and many clients.

There are two services offered by Windows Azure for message queues. This chapter covers Windows Azure queue. The other service is called 'Service Bus queue'.

Decoupling the components is one of the advantages of message queue services. It runs in an asynchronous environment where messages can be sent among the different components of an application. Thus, it provides an efficient solution for managing workflows and tasks. For example, a message to complete a task is sent from the frontend of the application and is received by a backend worker, who then completes the task and deletes the message.

Considerations

The messages in the storage queue are not replicated anywhere, that means there is only one copy of your message. The maximum number of messages that can be processed are 20,000. The maximum size of a message can be 40 kb.

Managing Queues using PowerShell
Create a Queue

Step 1 – Right-click on Windows PowerShell in the taskbar. Choose 'Run ISE as administrator'.

Step 2 – Run the following command to access your account. Please replace the highlighted part for your account.

```
$context = New-AzureStorageContext -StorageAccountName
    tutorialspoint StorageAccountKey
    iUZNeeJD+ChFHt9XHL6D5rkKFWjzyW4FhV0iLyvweDi+Xtzfy76juPzJ+mWt
    DmbqCWjsu/nr+1pqBJj rd002+A==
```

Step 3 – Specify the storage account in which you want to create a queue.

```
Set-AzureSubscription -SubscriptionName "BizSpark" -
    CurrentStorageAccount tutorialspoint
```

Step 4 – Create a Queue.

```
$QueueName = "thisisaqueue"
    $Queue = New-AzureStorageQueue –Name $QueueName -Context
    $Ctx
```

Retrieve a Queue

```
$QueueName = "thisisaqueue"

$Queue = Get-AzureStorageQueue –Name $QueueName –Context
$Ctx
```

Delete a Queue

```
$QueueName = "thisisaqueue"

Remove-AzureStorageQueue –Name $QueueName –Context $Ctx
```

Insert a Message into a Queue

Step 1 – Login to your account.

```
$context = New-AzureStorageContext -StorageAccountName
    tutorialspoint StorageAccountKey

    iUZNeeJD+ChFHt9XHL6D5rkKFWjzyW4FhV0iLyvweDi+Xtzfy76juPzJ+mWt
    DmbqCWjsu/nr+1pqBJj rdOO2+A==
```

Step 2 – Specify the storage account you want to use.

```
Set-AzureSubscription –SubscriptionName "BizSpark" -

    CurrentStorageAccount tutorialspoint
```

Step 3 – Retrieve the queue and then insert the message.

```
$QueueName = "myqueue"
   $Queue = Get-AzureStorageQueue -Name $QueueName -Context
   $ctx

   if ($Queue -ne $null) {
      $QueueMessage = New-Object -TypeName
   Microsoft.WindowsAzure.Storage.Queue.CloudQueueMessage
         -ArgumentList "my message is this"
      $Queue.CloudQueue.AddMessage($QueueMessage)
   }
```

The 'if' condition in the script above checks if the queue specified exists or not.

Dequeue Next Message from Queue

Step 1 – First connect to your account and specify the storage account, by running the commands as shown in the above steps.

Step 2 – Retrieve the queue.

```
$QueueName = "myqueue"
   $Queue = Get-AzureStorageQueue -Name $QueueName -Context
   $ctx
   $InvisibleTimeout = [System.TimeSpan]::FromSeconds(10)
```

Step 3 – Dequeue the next message.

```
$QueueMessage = $Queue.CloudQueue.GetMessage($InvisibleTimeout)
```

Step 4 – Delete the dequeued message.

```
$Queue.CloudQueue.DeleteMessage($QueueMessage)
```

Managing Queues using Azure Storage Explorer

Step 1 − Select the storage account from the dropdown at the top right. Accounts will be displayed if you have added them during your previous use. If not, you can add account and it will ask for your credentials. After signing in, you will be logged into your account in Azure Storage Explorer.

Step 2 − You can add a new queue by selecting 'Queues' from the left panel and clicking 'New' as shown in the following image.

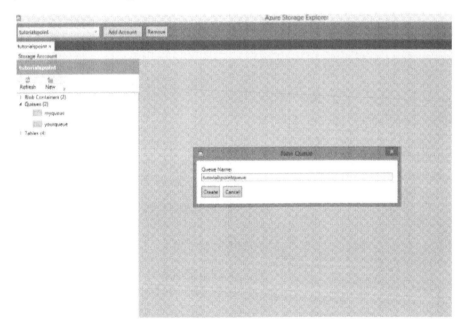

Step 3 − Enter the name of Queue and it is created in your storage account.

Step 4 – Add and delete the messages by selecting the queue in the left panel.

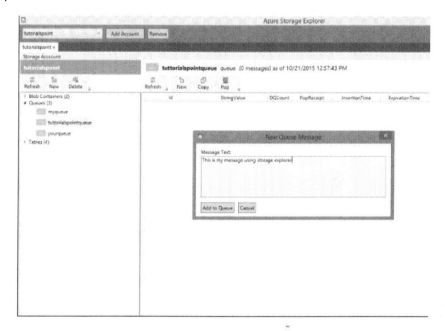

Microsoft Azure - Tables

Storing a table does not mean relational database here. Azure Storage can store just a table without any foreign keys or any other kind of relation. These tables are highly scalable and ideal for handling large amount of data. Tables can be stored and queried for large amount of data. The relational database can be stored using SQL Data Services, which is a separate service.

The three main parts of service are –

- Tables
- Entities
- Properties

For example, if 'Book' is an entity, its properties will be Id, Title, Publisher, Author etc. Table will be created for a collection of entities. There can be 252 custom properties and 3 system properties. An entity will always have system properties which are PartitionKey, RowKey and Timestamp. Timestamp is system generated but you will have to specify the PartitionKey and RowKey while inserting data into the table. The example below will make it clearer. Table name and Property name is case sensitive which should always be considered while creating a table.

How to Manage Tables Using PowerShell

Step 1 – Download and install Windows PowerShell as discussed previously in the tutorial.

Step 2 – Right-click on 'Windows PowerShell', choose 'Pin to Taskbar' to pin it on the taskbar of your computer.

Step 3 – Choose 'Run ISE as Administrator'.

Creating a Table

Step 1 – Copy the following commands and paste into the screen. Replace the highlighted text with your account.

Step 2 – Login into your account.

```
$StorageAccountName = "mystorageaccount"
$StorageAccountKey = "mystoragekey"
$Ctx = New-AzureStorageContext $StorageAccountName -
StorageAccountKey
$StorageAccountKey
```

Step 3 – Create a new table.

```
$tabName = "Mytablename"
New-AzureStorageTable –Name $tabName –Context $Ctx
```

The following image shows a table being created by the name of 'book'.

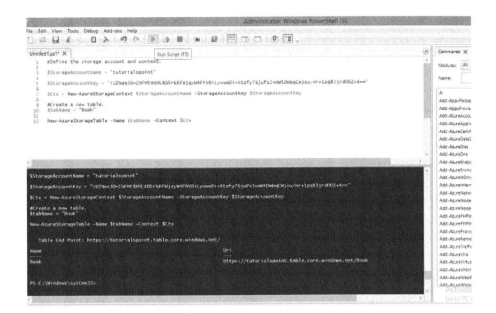

You can see that it has given the following end point as a result.

https://tutorialspoint.table.core.windows.net/Book

Similarly, you can retrieve, delete and insert data into the table using preset commands in PowerShell.

Retrieve Table

```
$tabName = "Book"
    Get-AzureStorageTable –Name $tabName –Context $Ctx
```

Delete Table

```
$tabName = "Book"
    Remove-AzureStorageTable –Name $tabName –Context $Ctx
```

Insert rows into Table

```
function Add-Entity() {
    [CmdletBinding()]

    param(
        $table,
        [String]$partitionKey,
        [String]$rowKey,
        [String]$title,
        [Int]$id,
        [String]$publisher,
        [String]$author
    )

    $entity = New-Object -TypeName
Microsoft.WindowsAzure.Storage.Table.DynamicTableEntity
        -ArgumentList $partitionKey, $rowKey

    $entity.Properties.Add("Title", $title)
    $entity.Properties.Add("ID", $id)
    $entity.Properties.Add("Publisher", $publisher)
    $entity.Properties.Add("Author", $author)


    $result = $table.CloudTable.Execute(
        [Microsoft.WindowsAzure.Storage.Table.TableOperation]
        ::Insert($entity))
}

$StorageAccountName = "tutorialspoint"
$StorageAccountKey = Get-AzureStorageKey -StorageAccountName
$StorageAccountName
$Ctx = New-AzureStorageContext $StorageAccountName -
StorageAccountKey
    $StorageAccountKey.Primary

$TableName = "Book"
```

```
$table = Get-AzureStorageTable -Name $TableName -Context
$Ctx -ErrorAction Ignore

#Add multiple entities to a table.
Add-Entity -Table $table -PartitionKey Partition1 -RowKey
Row1 -Title .Net -Id 1
   -Publisher abc -Author abc
Add-Entity -Table $table -PartitionKey Partition2 -RowKey
Row2 -Title JAVA -Id 2
   -Publisher abc -Author abc
Add-Entity -Table $table -PartitionKey Partition3 -RowKey
Row3 -Title PHP -Id 3
   -Publisher xyz -Author xyz
Add-Entity -Table $table -PartitionKey Partition4 -RowKey
Row4 -Title SQL -Id 4
   -Publisher xyz -Author xyz
```

Retrieve Table Data

```
$StorageAccountName = "tutorialspoint"
$StorageAccountKey = Get-AzureStorageKey -
StorageAccountName $StorageAccountName
$Ctx = New-AzureStorageContext - StorageAccountName
$StorageAccountName -
   StorageAccountKey $StorageAccountKey.Primary;

$TableName = "Book"

#Get a reference to a table.
$table = Get-AzureStorageTable -Name $TableName -Context
$Ctx

#Create a table query.
$query = New-Object
Microsoft.WindowsAzure.Storage.Table.TableQuery
```

```
#Define columns to select.
$list = New-Object System.Collections.Generic.List[string]
$list.Add("RowKey")
$list.Add("ID")
$list.Add("Title")
$list.Add("Publisher")
$list.Add("Author")

#Set query details.
$query.FilterString = "ID gt 0"
$query.SelectColumns = $list
$query.TakeCount = 20

#Execute the query.
$entities = $table.CloudTable.ExecuteQuery($query)

#Display entity properties with the table format.

$entities   | Format-Table PartitionKey, RowKey, @{ Label =
"Title";
Expression={$_.Properties["Title"].StringValue}}, @{ Label =
"ID";
Expression={$_.Properties["ID"].Int32Value}}, @{ Label =
"Publisher";
Expression={$_.Properties["Publisher"].StringValue}}, @{
Label = "Author";
Expression={$_.Properties["Author"].StringValue}} -AutoSize
```

The output will be as shown in the following image.

Delete Rows from Table

```
$StorageAccountName = "tutorialspoint"

$StorageAccountKey = Get-AzureStorageKey -
StorageAccountName $StorageAccountName
$Ctx = New-AzureStorageContext - StorageAccountName
$StorageAccountName -
    StorageAccountKey $StorageAccountKey.Primary

#Retrieve the table.
$TableName = "Book"
$table = Get-AzureStorageTable -Name $TableName -Context
$Ctx -ErrorAction
Ignore

#If the table exists, start deleting its entities.
if ($table -ne $null) {
    #Together the PartitionKey and RowKey uniquely identify
every
```

```
#entity within a table.

$tableResult = $table.CloudTable.Execute(
    [Microsoft.WindowsAzure.Storage.Table.TableOperation]
    ::Retrieve("Partition1", "Row1"))

$entity = $tableResult.Result;

if ($entity -ne $null) {
    $table.CloudTable.Execute(

[Microsoft.WindowsAzure.Storage.Table.TableOperation]
        ::Delete($entity))
    }
}
```

The above script will delete the first row from the table, as you can see that we have specified Partition1 and Row1 in the script. After you are done with deleting the row, you can check the result by running the script for retrieving rows. There you will see that the first row is deleted.

While running these commands please ensure that you have replaced the accountname with your account name, accountkey with your account key.

How to Manage Table using Azure Storage Explorer

Step 1 – Login in to your Azure account and go to your storage account.

Step 2 – Click on the link 'Storage explorer' as shown in purple circle in the following image.

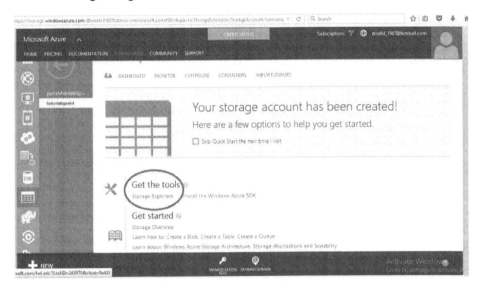

Step 3 – Choose 'Azure Storage Explorer for Windows' from the list. It is a free tool that you can download and install on your computer.

Step 4 – Run this program on your computer and click 'Add Account' button at the top.

Step 5 – Enter 'Storage Account Name' and 'Storage account Key' and click 'Test Access. The buttons are encircled in following image.

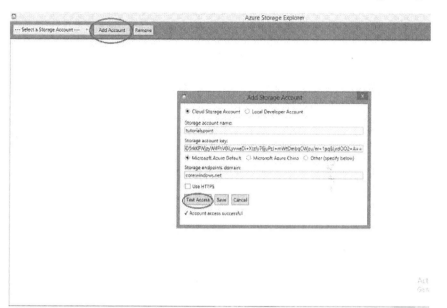

Step 6 – If you already have any tables in storage you will see in the left panel under 'Tables'. You can see the rows by clicking on them.

Create a Table

Step 1 – Click on 'New' and enter the table name as shown in the following image.

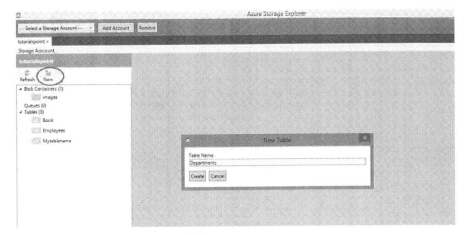

Insert Row into Table

Step 1 – Click on 'New'.

Step 2 – Enter Field Name.

Step 3 – Select data type from dropdown and enter field value.

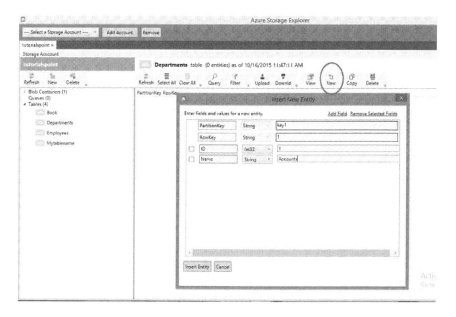

Step 4 – To see the rows created click on the table name in the left panel.

Azure Storage Explorer is very basic and easy interface to manage tables. You can easily create, delete, upload, and download tables using this interface. This makes the tasks very easy for developers as compared to writing lengthy scripts in Windows PowerShell.

Microsoft Azure - CDN

Caching is one of the ways for performance improvement. Windows Azure uses caching to increase the speed of cloud services. Content Delivery Management (CDN) puts stuff like blobs and other static content in a cache. The process involves placing the data at strategically chosen locations and caching it. As a result, it provides maximum bandwidth for its delivery to users. Let's assume an application's source is far away from the end user and many tours are taken over the internet to fetch data; the CDN offers a very competent solution to improve performance in this case. Additionally, it scales the instant high load in a very efficient manner.

Create a CDN

Step 1 – Login in to your Azure Management Portal.

Step 2 – Click on 'New' at bottom left corner.

Step 3 – Select 'APP Services' then 'CDN'.

Step 4 – Click on 'Quick Create'. The following screen will come up.

You will see three fields in the pop up –

- **Subscription** – There will be a list of subscriptions you have subscribed to and you can choose from one of them. In this demo, only one option was there in the subscription dropdown, which was 'BizSpark', the current subscription.

- **Origin Type** – This dropdown will ask to select an origin type. The integrated service will have an option of Web Apps, Cloud Services, Storage and Media Services.

- **Origin URL** – This will show the URLs based on the chosen origin type in the dropdown.

Step 5 – Choose one of the options from each dropdown as needed and click 'Create'. CDN endpoint is created as show in the following image.

Create CDN for Custom Origin Links

In June 2015, CDN was updated with one more feature where users can specify a custom origin. Earlier only Azure services could be linked to CDN, but now any website can be linked to it using this service.

When we are create a CDN service, in the 'Origin Type' dropdown, there is an option 'Custom Origin' as shown in the following image, and then you can specify the link in the URL field.

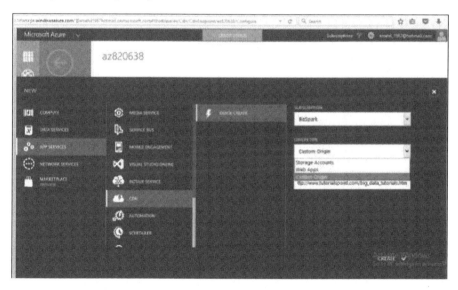

Manage CDN

Step 1 — Click on the Name of the CDN you want to manage in the list displayed in CDN **services**.

Step 2 — Click on 'manage cdn'.

Country filtering — You can allow/bock your website in specified countries. This is going to protect your data for better.

Step 3 — When you click on 'manage cdn' you will be taken to the following page in a new tab of your browser.

Step 4 — Click on 'Country Filtering' from menu items at the top of screen. Click on 'Add Country Filter' button as shown in the following image.

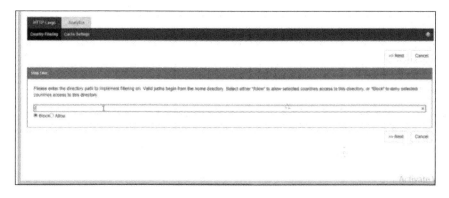

Step 5 – Specify the directory and select Allow/block.

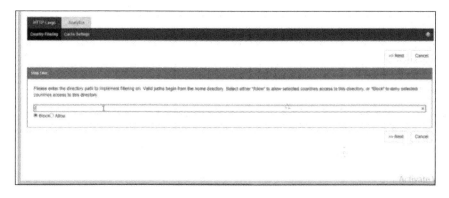

Step 6 – Select the country in the next screen and you are done.

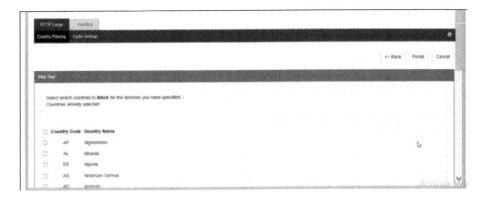

Compression – It allows files to be compressed. You can enable/disable compression. Also you can specify the file type.

Step 7 – Click on 'Cache Setting' and scroll down to the bottom of the page.

Step 8 – Select 'Compression Enabled' and click 'Update' button. By default, compression is disabled.

Analytics – You can see very useful figures in this section. For example, number of overall hits or in a specific geographic region. The report will also show how many times requests are served from CDN endpoints and how many of them are going back to the original server.

Step 9 – Click on 'Analytics' in menu items at the top of the page. You will see a list of all the reports in the left panel as shown in the following image.

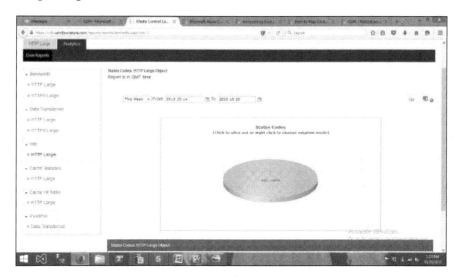

Step 10 – Additionally, you can download the report as an excel file by clicking on the excel icon at the top right corner.

Map a Custom Domain Name

You might want to use a custom domain name instead of CDN endpoint that is autogenerated by Azure service. Windows Azure has provided a new feature that allows you to map a custom domain name to his application's CDN endpoint. Let's see how it is done in Azure Portal.

Step 1 – Click on 'Manage Domain' Button on the bottom horizontal menu.

Step 2 – Enter the custom URL in the text box and its done.

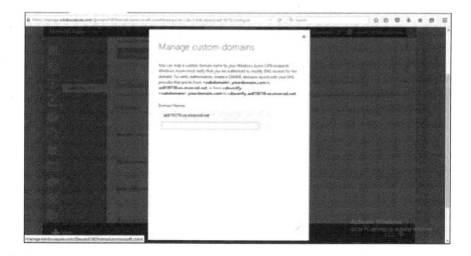

Microsoft Azure - Applications

Windows Azure is usually misinterpreted as just a hosting solution, but there is a lot more that can be done using Windows Azure. It provides a platform to develop applications using a range of available technologies and programming languages. It offers to create and deploy applications using .net platform, which is Microsoft's own application development technology. In addition to .net, there are many more technologies and languages supported. For example, Java, PHP, Ruby, Oracle, Linux, MySQL, Python.

Windows Azure applications are scaled by creating multiple instances of the application. The number of instances needed by the application is specified by the developer while hosting the applications. If traffic is increased or decreased on the website or web application it can be managed easily by logging in to Windows Azure management portal and specifying the instances. Load balancing can also be automated which would allow Azure to make the decision itself as when to assign more resources to application.

Web applications support .net, java, python, php and node.js. Tasks such as scaling and backups can be easily automated. A new feature called 'webjobs' is available, which is a kind of batch processing service. Webjobs can also be scaled and scheduled. The mobile application platforms supported are Xamarin iOS, Xamarin Android and IOS.

Azure platform is developed in such a way that developers need to concentrate on only the development part and need not worry about other technical stuff outside their domain. Thus most of the administrative work is done by Azure itself.

A marketplace is also set by Azure where its customers can buy applications and services. It is a platform where customers can search applications and deploy them in an easier way. Azure marketplace is available in 88 countries at present. An application purchased from the marketplace can be easily connected to the local development environment by the application developers. The pricing is done using 5 different models, which includes usage-based and monthly fee. Some of the applications are even free of charge.

Microsoft Azure - Security

Security is about managing the access of users to the organization's applications, platforms and portals. Active directory is used to manage the database of users in a protected manner. The same kind of service is provided by Windows Azure to keep the users and their password safe. Active directory is a feature that lets you create users, manage their roles, grant access and delete them.

Creating an Active Directory

Step 1 – Sign in to Azure Management Portal.

Step 2 – Click 'New' and then click 'App Services'.

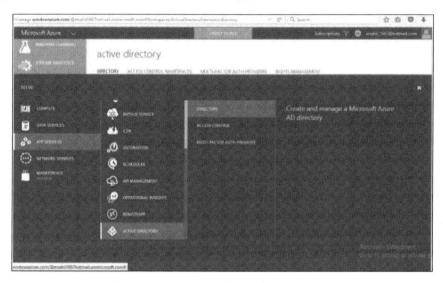

Step 3 – Click 'Active Directory' and then 'Directory'.

Step 4 – Click 'Custom Create'.

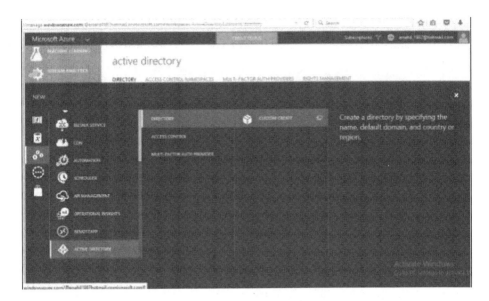

Step 5 — Enter the details and you are done. In the following image, 'tutpoint' is the domain name. Enter a domain name which is a temporary DNS. Once its directory is created, you can map it to your own domain.

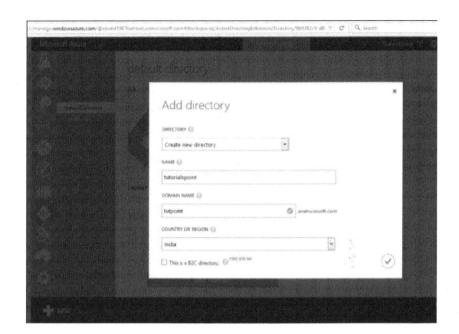

Mapping a Custom Domain

Since you have provided a temporary domain name, when creating a directory in Windows Azure, you can map it to your own domain using this functionality.

Step 1 – Click on the directory name in the list of your directory.

Step 2 – Click on 'Domains' from the top menu items.

Step 3 – Click 'Add a Custom Domain'.

Step 4 – In the screen that pops up, enter the details. You can choose for 'single sign in option' if needed.

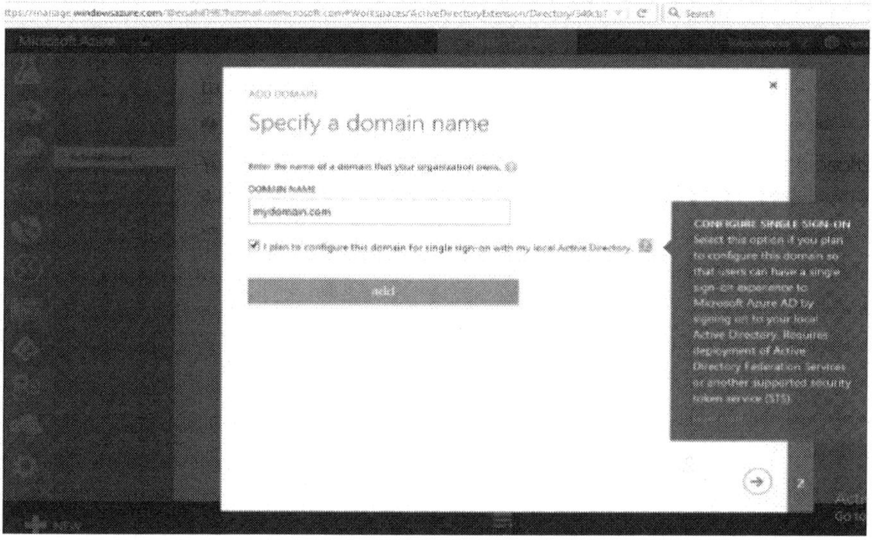
ADD DOMAIN
Specify a domain name
Enter the name of a domain that your organization owns.
DOMAIN NAME
mydomain.com
I plan to configure this domain for single sign-on with my local Active Directory.
add
CONFIGURE SINGLE SIGN-ON
Select this option if you plan to configure this domain so that users can have a single sign-on experience to Microsoft Azure AD by signing on to your local Active Directory. Requires deployment of Active Directory Federation Services or another supported security token service (STS).

Creating Users

Step 1 – Click on 'Add User' button at the bottom of the screen.

Step 2 – The following screen pops up. You can create a new user or link an existing Microsoft account. You can even import a user from other directory in Azure. Let's choose 'Create a new user' here.

Step 3 − Enter the user name in the following screen.

Step 4 − Enter other details and choose the role for the user.

Step 5 — Click next arrow and it will create a user for your application and give you a temporary password which can be changed by the user.

Integrating with Azure Active Directory

Step 1 – Locate and click 'Application' at top of screen.

Step 2 – Click on 'Add' displayed at the bottom of the screen. A pop up shown in the following image will be seen on the screen.

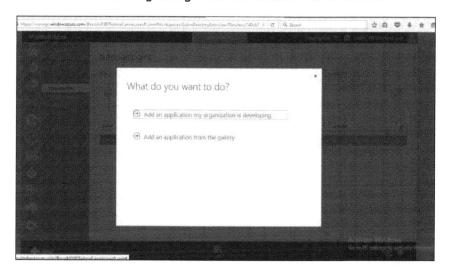

Step 3 – If you click the first option, it will take you to the following screen. You can enter the name of the application and follow the wizard.

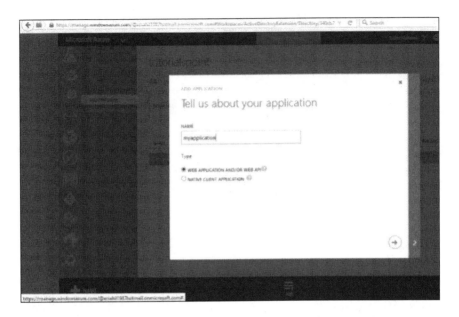

Step 4 – Similarly, if you choose the second option in 'What do you want to do' pop up, it will let you choose an application from the gallery as shown in the following screen.

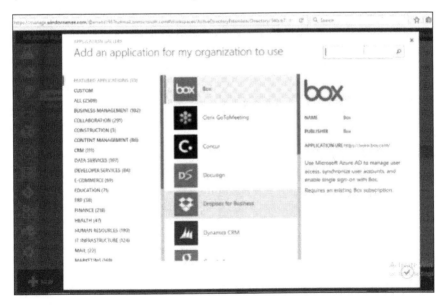

Integrating On-Premise Active Directory

Azure active directory lets you run an active directory in cloud and also lets you connect it to your on-premise active directory. Basically, it will replicate your user database residing on your on-premise machine in cloud. It will also automatically synchronize whenever changes are made on-premise.

Click on the 'Directory Integration' from the top menu. An on-premise directory can be connected using the three steps as shown in the following image.

Reports

This is a very useful feature of Active Directory as it shows different reports such as number of times a user is signing in, or signing in from an unknown device can be seen here.

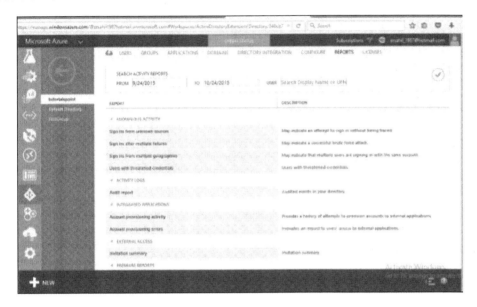

Microsoft Azure - Datacenters

When we think of cloud, we imagine a place with large number of machines in big rooms. There must be a place where all the data is stored. Microsoft has datacenters all over the world from where Windows Azure services are managed. Datacenters are divided in regions. The exact location of these datacenters is not revealed by Microsoft for obvious security reasons.

Following are the 20 listed regions as can also be seen in the image.

- Central US
- East US
- East US 2
- US Gov Iowa
- US Gov Virginia
- North Central US
- South Central US
- West US
- North Europe
- West Europe
- East Asia
- Southeast Asia

- Japan East

- Japan West

- Brazil South

- Australia East

- Australia Southeast

- Central India

- South India

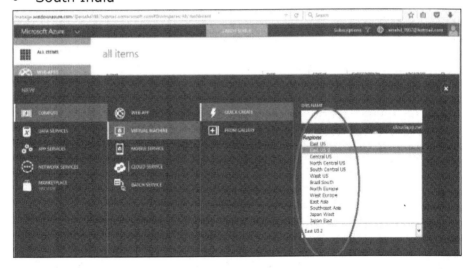

How to Choose the Right Data Center for Your Application

When creating Windows Azure application, whether it is mobile application, web application or database storage it asks to specify the region. Region here specifies a regional datacenter.

Performance – You should select the nearest datacenter to the users of your application. The performance can be affected by the relative location of the users who want to access the application. If a user is closer to the datacenter, the performance will be better.

Cost – The price of hosting the application may also increase or decrease depending upon the datacenter you choose. Price actually can vary according to the database hosting location or any other service being used by the application. You should choose the same location for all the services that are being used by your application. For example, database or any media service. If they are kept in separate datacenter there will be charges per transaction, but anything extra won't be charged if they are kept at the same datacenter.

Legal Aspect – Laws vary from country to country and restrictions could be enforced in some regions on what information can be shared and what cannot.

Microsoft Azure - Scenarios

Understanding the basic scenarios of Windows Azure will help us understand its use. Additionally, it will help us understand the services offered. Three basic scenarios are discussed here. In addition to the following scenarios, there can be many more ways of using Azure services based on the needs of clients, but all the basic uses are covered in this chapter.

Software Development

Software development is the most popular scenario of Windows Azure. The software is developed and tested on local development fabric and then deployed in cloud of Windows Azure. Azure hosts the web application and also the supporting processes, communicating with other web services.

Testing of application in software development phase usually becomes too long for developers, if they need to change the configurations of environment being used to host the application. In Windows Azure, this is the not a problem as resources are absolutely in their control and can be modified as needed by the application. Once a web application is hosted in cloud of Windows Azure, it is ready to be used by the end users and organizations.

Moreover, deploying the application is very easy in Windows Azure using the tools provided by them. These tools are MS deploy, PowerShell, integration with Team Foundation Server (TFS). The Visual Studio cloud project is also an easy option to deploy the application.

An application is tested in the staging environment and then it is deployed in the production environment for end users to use it.

Enterprise Process Offloading

There are situations for an organization where they need to reduce loads from their onpremise systems for a certain period of time or on a regular basis. This could be easily achieved by using Windows Azure services at a very low cost. Clients have to pay for only those transactions made on their application instead of paying for entire hardware and software.

This is an extremely cost-efficient way of using new resources for the organization. Azure in this context offers quite quick growth to businesses by extending resources on cloud when needed.

Enterprise Application Integration

This is commonly called as EAI scenario. Let us think of a scenario, when there is need for two different organizations to send and receive data between applications which is further processed by those applications. The cross-enterprise application integration can be done using Windows Azure. The service is called BizTalk service, which facilitates B2B messaging between on-premise or on-cloud applications of different organizations.

This service enables a connection between applications even if they are following different transport protocols. The process also includes validating and extracting the properties as required by the application at the receiving end. In a normal scenario, where communication is needed between applications of two organizations, the interaction will have to bypass the firewall by completing the due process. However, in the service offered by Windows Azure, the communication between applications does not need to bypass the organization's firewall.

Microsoft Azure - Management Portal

As the name suggests this is a portal to manage Azure services, which was released in 2012. This is a platform provided by Microsoft for its Azure clients where they can see, manage and buy the services offered by Azure. A different portal called 'Azure Preview Portal' was released by Azure team in 2014, which makes it easier to access the platform on mobiles and tablets. However, features are more or less same in both the portals.

To access the management portal –

Step 1 – Go to https://manage.windowsazure.com

Step 2 – Sign in with your Hotmail or live ID. If you don't have Azure accounts, sign up for one. You will get a free trial and you can explore, learn and create your own applications using Windows Azure.

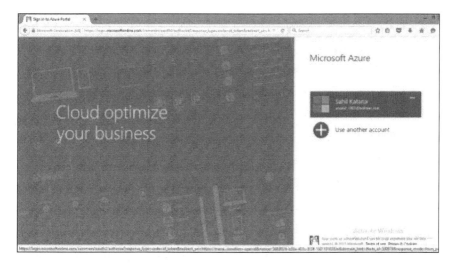

The following screen will appear.

Since here we have an application already running, you can see a list of them. Your account will be empty for the first time. Left panel categorizes the application and the middle part lists all the application in the account.

Create a New Application

Step 1 – Click on the 'New' left bottom corner.

Step 2 – Following screen will come up and you can choose what you want to create.

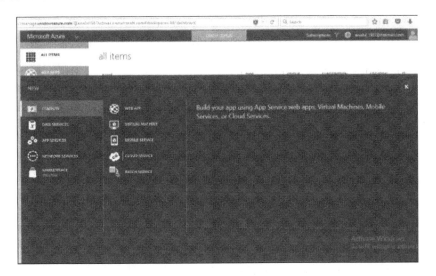

Check Credit and Subscriptions

Step 1 – Click on 'Credit' in the green block at the top of the screen.

Step 2 – Click on 'View more details'. It will take you to the following screen. This screen will show you all the details of your subscription, spending, and data usage.

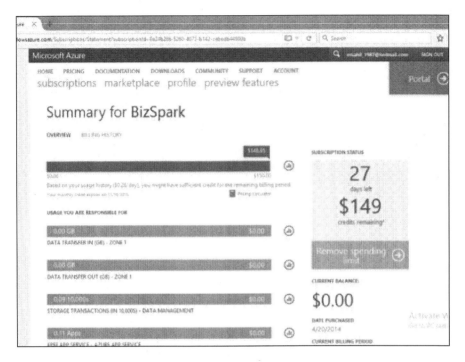

As the spending limit is set here, it says 'Remove Spending Limit'. If the limit would not have been set, it would have said 'Set Spending Limit'. This way you can set a spending limit for you. Your services will be stopped once you reach the spending limit.

If you scroll down on the page in the above image, you can see all that is available with your subscription and see the details on the right side.

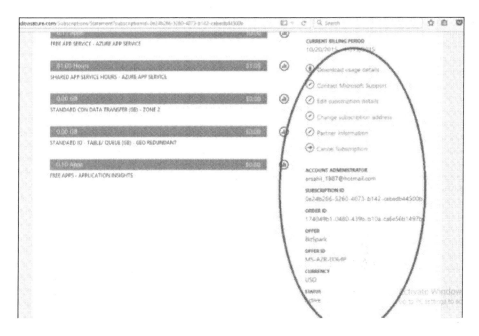

You are absolutely in control of your spending. The green block in which 'Credit' button is displayed will change color if you are about to fall short of your credit. This is calculated by your average per day spending and it would tell you in how many days your credit is going to get over.

Add a New Subscription

Step 1 – Click on your account e-mail id or on the picture at the top right corner.

Step 2 – Click on 'View my bill' in the list.

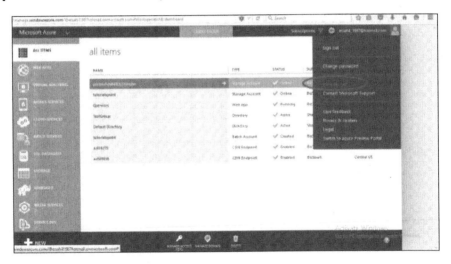

Step 3 – It will take you the following screen. Click on 'add subscription'.

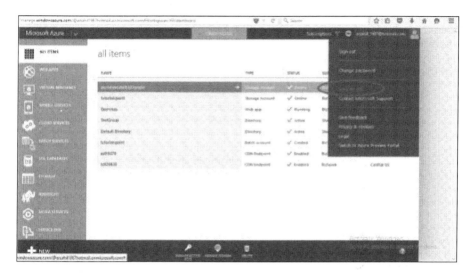

Step 4 – Choose the subscription from the list in the following screen.

Azure Preview Portal

Step 1 – Click on your account e-mail at the top right corner.

Step 2 – Select 'Switch to Azure Preview Portal'.

Step 3 – The following screen will appear. All the functionalities are same. 'Azure Preview Portal' is built for mobile and tablet screen with a responsive design.

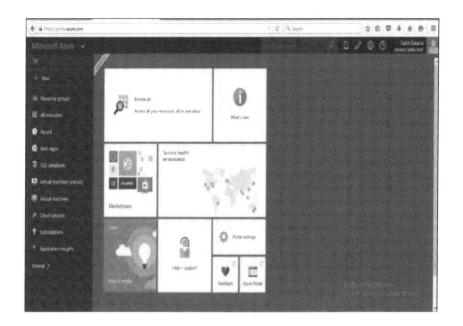

Microsoft Azure - Create Virtual Network

You can create virtual network on cloud or you can also connect to the on-premise local network to the cloud network in Windows Azure. This tutorial will first explain how to create a cloud only network.

Creating a Virtual Network in Clouds Only

Step 1 – Login in to Azure Management Portal.

Step 2 – Click on 'New' at the bottom left corner.

Step 3 – Click on 'Network Services' and then 'Virtual Network'.

Step 4 – Click on 'Quick Create'.

Step 5 – Enter the name and leave all other fields as they are except location. You don't need to specify anything in this case since everything will be decided by Azure itself.

Step 6 – Click on 'Create a Virtual Network' and it is done.

Creating a Virtual Network in Cloud Only (Advanced Settings)

Step 1 – Click on 'custom create' instead of 'quick create' when creating a new virtual network and the following screen will appear.

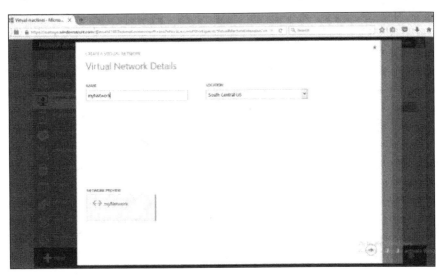

Step 2 – Enter the name of the 'Network' and choose a location. You will see that it will draw an image at the bottom.

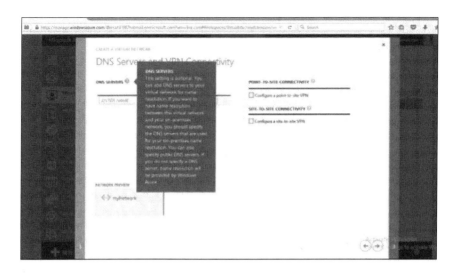

DNS Server Name is optional to enter as we are creating a cloud only network. Also, leave the options 'Point to Site connectivity' and 'Site to Site connectivity' as they are. The subsequent chapters will have a demo on configuration of these two options.

Step 3 – Click next and leave the default values on the following screen.

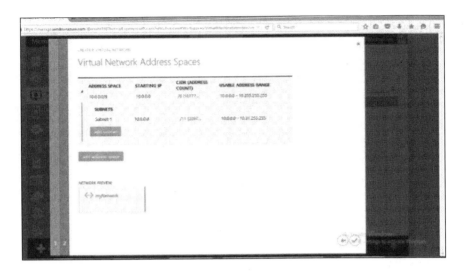

Step 4 – Click the next arrow and a virtual network is created.

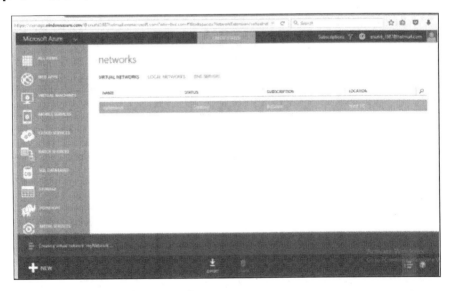

You can add DNS servers and local network even after creating a virtual network.

Microsoft Azure - Deploying Virtual Machines

A quick process of creating a virtual machine was included in the chapter 'Compute Module'. This chapter contains the detailed process including how to configure virtual machines.

Quick Create

Step 1 – Login to Azure Management Portal.

Step 2 – Locate and click on 'Virtual Machines' in the left panel and then click on 'Create a Virtual Machine'.

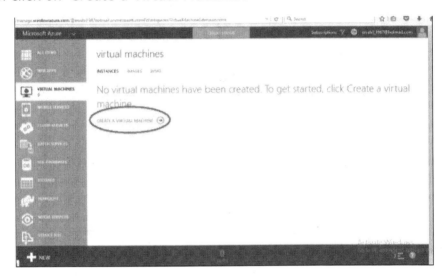

Step 3 – Alternatively, click 'New' at the bottom left corner and then click 'Compute' → 'Virtual Machine' →'Quick Create'.

Step 4 – Enter DNS name. This has to be unique. The DNS name is used to connect to the virtual machine.

Step 5 – Select the image and size from the dropdown list. The size affects the cost of running virtual machine.

Step 6 – Enter username and password. You must remember to log in to the virtual machine later.

Step 7 – Select the relevant region.

Step 8 – Click on 'Create a virtual machine' and you are ready to use your new machine. It will take a few seconds for the machine to be created.

Create Virtual Machine with Advanced Settings

Step 1 – Choose 'Custom Create' instead of 'Quick Create' in the options and you will be taken to the following screen.

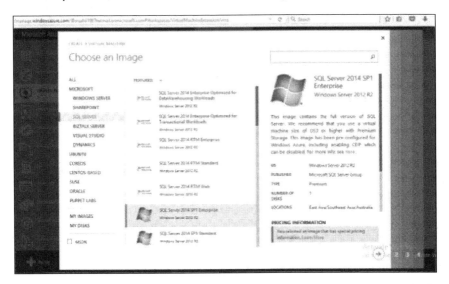

Step 2 – Choose an image from the list. In this screen, you find that choosing an image is easier based on their category shown on the left side. Let us create a virtual machine for SQL Server for which we have chosen SQL Server on the left side and all the software in this category are shown in the middle.

Step 3 – Click on the Next arrow.

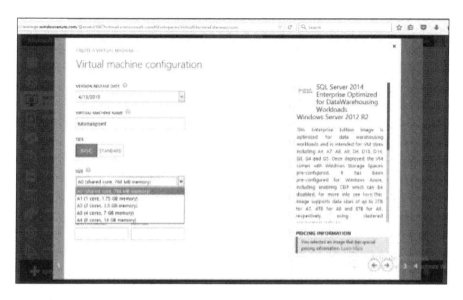

Step 4 – Choose Version Release Date and enter the VM's name.

Step 5 – Select the Tier. The size dropdown would change items according to tier. In the basic version, you will get only first 5 options, while in the standard version you will get more options. It should be according to you and you image's requirements. For example, in this case let's choose SQL server. It requires minimum A4 machine with 8 cores and 14GB memory.

Step 6 – Enter the username and password and click Next arrow.

Step 7 – Enter DNS name which should be unique as mentioned earlier and select the region.

Under the storage account, it will display the storage accounts that you have already created. As seen in the following screen, an account name is shown in the dropdown which is a storage account created earlier. You can choose an already created account or even use an automatically generated account.

Step 8 – Next is Availability set. This option lets you create a set of virtual machines that will ensure that if a single point fails, it doesn't affect your machine and keeps the work going on. Let's choose the option 'none' here.

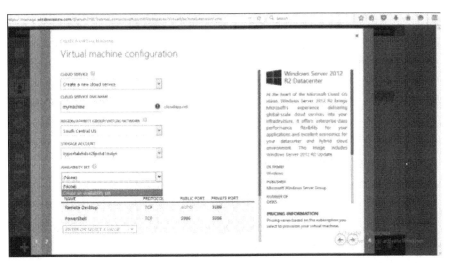

The last option is End Points. End points are used to communicate with virtual machines by other resources you can leave. In a subsequent chapter, we will provide a detailed illustration to configure endpoints.

Step 9 − Click on Next and the virtual machine will be created in a few seconds for you.

Connecting with a Virtual Network

Step 1 – Create a virtual machine using the steps described earlier. If you already have a virtual network created in Azure, it will be diplayed in the highlighted dropdown list as shown in the following screen. You can choose the network as shown in following picture.

Step 2 – When you go to your Virtual Network and management portal created earlier, click on 'Dashboard'. The virtual machine will be displyed in the resources of that network as shown in the following picture.

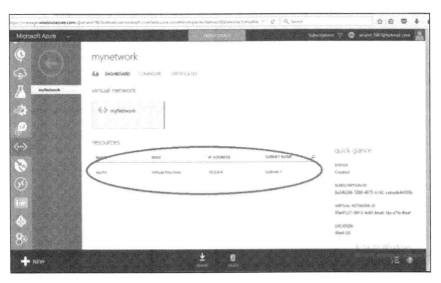

Accessing the Virtual Machine

There is a step by step guide on connecting to VM in 'Compute Module' chapter earlier in this tutorial. Please refer to it.

Considerations

While creating a virtual machine following considerations should be made –

- Choose the location according to the user's location to avoid any latency issues. It is best to choose the region nearest to the physical location of end users.

- You must go through the costs that will be incurred based on the size you choose for the virtual machine beforehand, to make sure it is in control.

- If you use the already created storage account you will be able to manage things better.

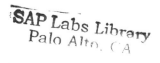

Microsoft Azure - Endpoint Configuration

When creating a virtual machine, we come across a part where endpoints can be configured. The two default endpoints enabled while creating a virtual machine are Remote Desktop and PowerShell. What actually is an endpoint? Virtual machine on same cloud can communicate to each other automatically. But in case we need them to communicate with our own computer, we will need an endpoint configured to make it happen. It is basically accessing the virtual machine through a port. An endpoint provides remote access to the services running on virtual machine. It has a public and private port that needs to be specified while creating an endpoint. Additionally, an endpoint can be accessed securely by activating Access Control Lists (ACL).

In the following section, it is demonstrated how a new endpoint can be configured for virtual machine that's already been created. However, it can also be done in the same way as creating a new one on configuration part of wizard.

Step 1 – Click on Virtual Machine in your Azure Management portal.

Step 2 – Click on 'Endpoint' and then Click on 'Add'.

Step 3 – Select 'Add a Stand-Alone Endpoint' as shown in the following image.

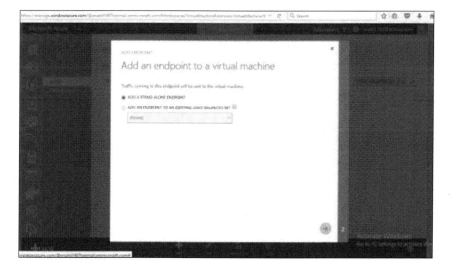

Step 4 – Select the name from dropdown. Alternatively, you can enter a custom name. Here let's select Http from options. It will assign unused ports automatically. Or you can enter it manually.

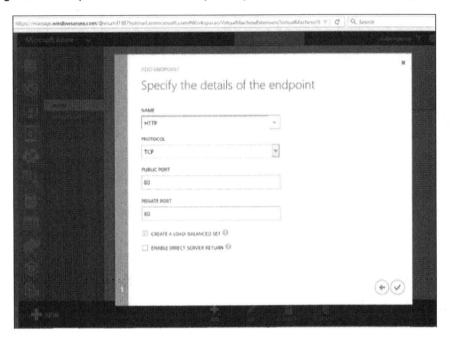

Step 5 – If you tick 'Create a Load Balanced Set', it will allow distributing the load across virtual machines. Let's leave it unchecked here because it can be configured later, if needed.

Step 6 – The 'Enable Direct Server Return' is checked when SQL server's 'Always On' feature is required, so let's leave it unchecked.

Step 7 – Click on Next arrow.

Access Control of Endpoint

We can grant or deny the access of services to an individual host or network. If nothing is specified, the endpoint can be accessed from any host and network.

Step 1 − Select 'Manage ACL' as shown in the following image.

Step 2 − Enter access description.

Step 3 − Enter Subnet Mask.

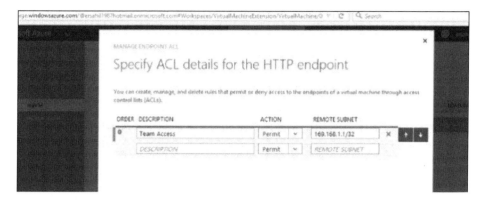

Step 4 — Click on Next and it's done.

Microsoft Azure - Point-to-Site Connectivity

In the last chapter, we saw how an endpoint can be created to access a virtual machine; this is quite a tedious task. If a virtual machine in virtual network needs to be connected with on-premise machine, the point-to-site connectivity is needed. Point-to-site connectivity makes it very productive to work with remote virtual machines.

Basically, a machine on-premise is connected to virtual network using point-to-site connectivity. However, we can connect up to 128 on-premise machines to virtual network in Azure. The access to the virtual network in cloud is granted through a certificate. The certificate has to be installed on each local machine that needs to be connected to the virtual network.

Enabling Point-to-Site Connectivity on Existing Virtual Network

If you have already created a virtual network in Azure, you can access it in management portal.

Step 1 – Log in to Azure management portal.

Step 2 – Click on 'Networks' in the left panel and select the network you want to work with.

Step 3 – Click on 'Configure' as shown in the following image.

Step 4 – Check the 'Configure Point-to-site connectivity' checkbox. It will allow you to enter the starting IP and CIDR.

Step 5 – Scroll down and click 'add gateway subnet'.

Step 6 – Enter the Gateway subnet and click 'Save'. Message shown in the following screen will pop up.

Step 7 – Click Yes and a point-to-site connectivity is done.

You will need a certificate to access your virtual network.

Create a New Virtual Network with Point-to-site Connectivity

Step 1 – Click New → Network Services → Virtual Network → Custom Create.

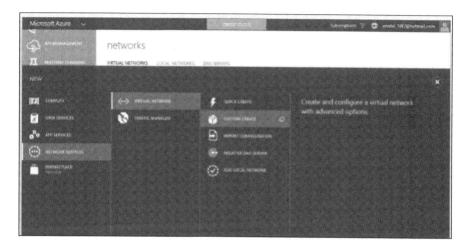

Step 2 – Enter Network's name, select location and click on Next.

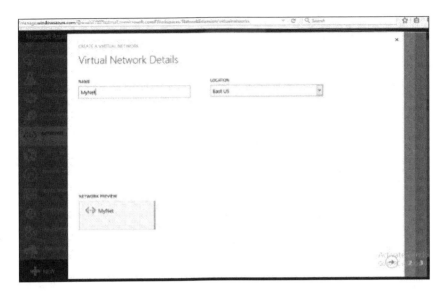

Step 3 – On the next screen, Select 'Configure a point-to-site VPN' and click next.

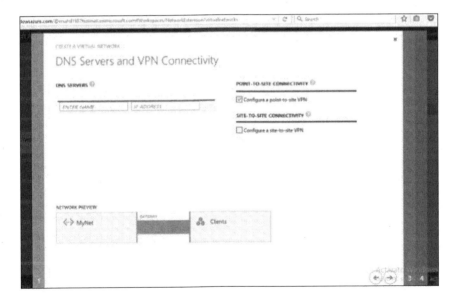

Step 4 – You can select or enter starting IP and select CIDR.

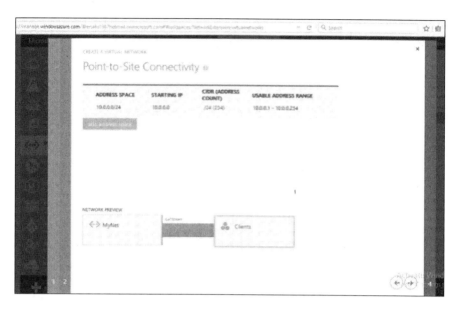

Step 5 — Enter Subnet and click 'Add Gateway Subnet' as done earlier and enter the required information.

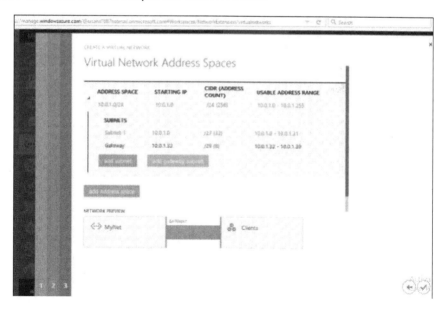

Step 6 — Point-to-Site connectivity is done.

Step 7 – Click on the name of the network, as it is 'MyNet' in the above image.

Step 8 – Click on 'Dashboard' as shown in the following screen.

You will see that the gateway is not created yet. For it to happen, you will have to generate a certificate first.

Generate Certificates

The point-to-site VPN supports only self-signed certificate.

Create a Certificate

Step 1 – Go to the link msdn.microsoft.com or google 'windows SDK for 8.1'. Then go to msdn link or the version of Windows for which you want the tool.

Step 2 – Download the encircled file as shown in the following image. It will be saved as .exe file named sdksetup on your machine.

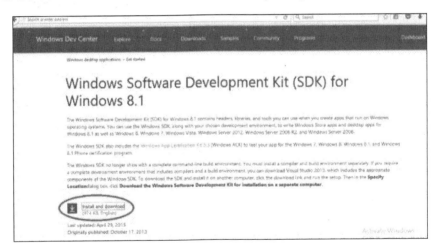

Step 3 – Run the file. While running the installation wizard, when you reach the following screen uncheck the encircled part. By default they are checked.

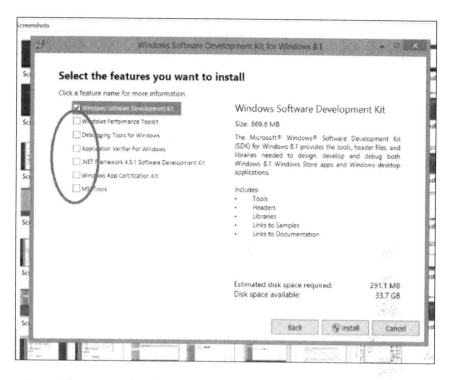

Step 4 – After installation is complete, run Command Prompt as Administrator on your computer.

Step 5 – Enter the following commands one by one for creating root certificate

```
cd C:\Program Files (x86)\Windows Kits\8.1\bin\x64
```

```
makecert -sky exchange -r -n "CN=MyNet" -pe -a sha1 -len 2048 -ss
My
```

First command will change the directory in command prompt. In the above command change the highlighted part to the name of your network.

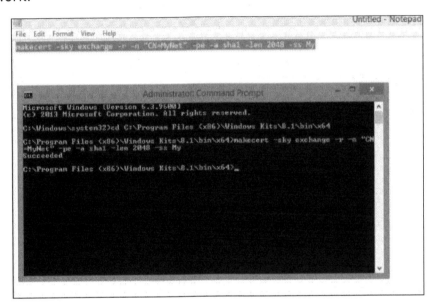

Step 6 – Next enter the following command for creating client certificate.

```
makecert -n "CN=MyNetClient" -pe -sky exchange -m 96 -ss My -in
    "MyNet" -is my -a sha1
```

Step 7 – Look for 'mmc' on your computer and run it.

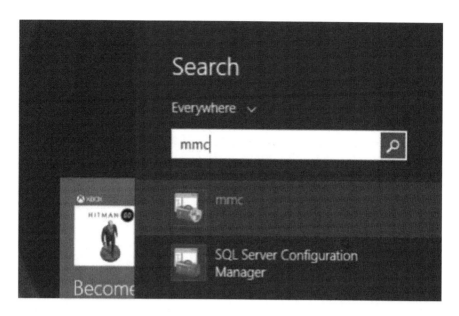

Step 8 – Click 'File' and 'Add/Remove Snap-in'.

Step 9 – In the screen that pops up, click 'Certificate' and then on 'add'.

Step 10 – Select 'My User Account' and click on 'Finish'.

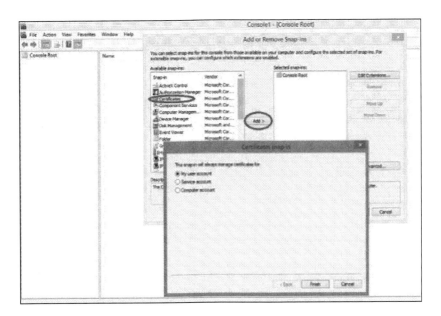

Step 11 – Expand 'Current User' in the left panel, then 'Personal' and then 'Certificates'.

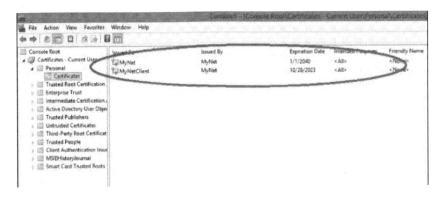

You can see the certificates here.

Step 12 – Right click on certificate and click 'All Tasks' and then 'Export'.

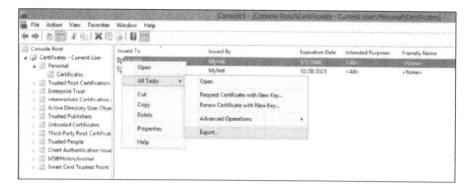

Step 13 — Follow the wizard. You will have to name the certificate and select a location to save it.

Upload the Certificate

Step 1 — Login to Azure management portal.

Step 2 — Go to the network and click 'Certificate' and then click 'Upload Root Certificate'.

Step 3 — Click browse and select the location of the certificate you just created.

Download the Client VPN Package

Client VPN Package will connect you to the network.

Step 1 — Go to network's dashboard in azure management portal.

Step 2 — Scroll down and locate the following options at the right side of the screen.

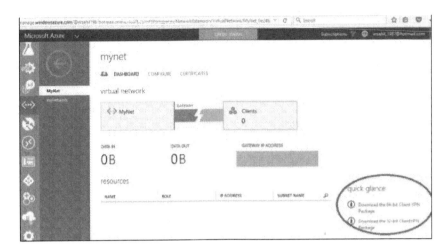

Step 3 – Select the suitable option and download it. You will see a similar file on your computer. Run and install it.

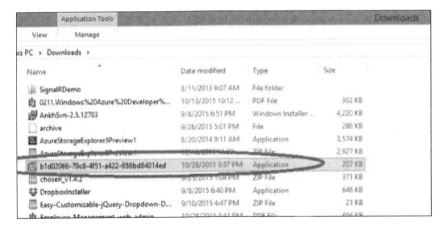

Step 4 – When you'll install it, Windows might try to prevent it. Choose 'Run Anyway' if this happens.

Step 5 – Go to 'Networks' on your machine and you will see a VPN connection available as shown in the following image.

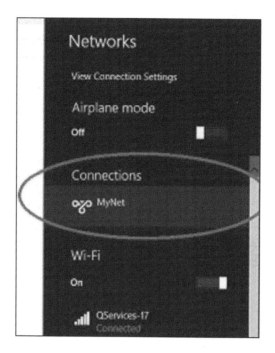

Step 6 – Click on that network as in this example 'MyNet' and connect. You will be connected to the network.

Microsoft Azure - Site-to-Site Connectivity

Most organizations already have a network on their premises and would want to connect it to Windows Azure rather than putting everything on cloud. It is also called hybrid network connectivity. It is connecting virtual net in Azure to on-premises network. Setting up a site-to-site connectivity network is quite easy for someone who knows the basics of networking like IPs, subnetting and default gateways.

The things that are required before configuring the network in this case are –

- A VPN device that can be configured.
- Externally facing IP address for that VPN device.

Creating a Site-to-Site Connectivity Network

Step 1 – Select New → Network Services → Virtual Network → Custom Create

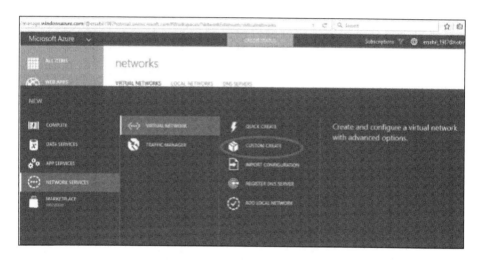

Step 2 – Enter the name of the network and select the region.

Step 3 – Enter the DNS name for name resolution if you want, otherwise you can leave it empty if you want it to be automatically done by Azure.

Step 4 – Check the 'Configure site-to-site VPN' option.

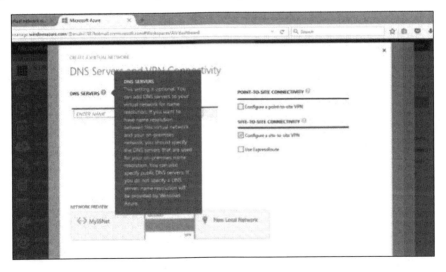

Step 5 – Enter the details of your VPN device in the address space as shown in the following image.

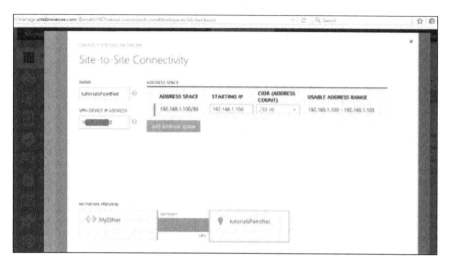

Step 6 – Enter the details of your virtual network in the address space.

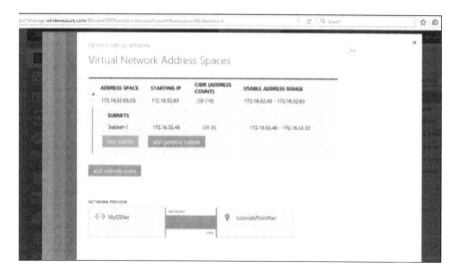

Step 7 – After entering the subnets, enter the gateway subnet for your virtual network.

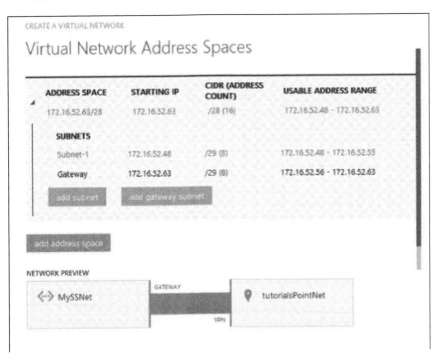

Step 8 – Click next and the network is created.

Step 9 – Select the network and go to its 'Dashboard'. You will have to create a gateway for it.

Step 10 – Click 'Create Gateway' at the bottom of the screen. Once gateway is created 'Gateway IP address' is displayed on the following screen.

You can configure the VPN device now using the information.

Site-to-site connectivity is faster than the point-to-site connectivity. It makes transferring of data easier. You just need a shared key to access the network. Unlike point-to-site connectivity, you don't have to install certificates on each machine you want to connect with the virtual machine. In fact, the same shared key works for each machine.

Microsoft Azure - Traffic Manager

Let us first understand what is the service provided by Azure traffic manager. Basically, this service balances the traffic load of services hosted in Azure. The routing policy is defined by the client and traffic to the services hosted in Azure is redirected according to set policies. Traffic manager is a DNS-based service. Thus, it will improve the availability and performance applications.

Let's see how to create and configure traffic manager in Azure.

Create Traffic Manager

Step 1 – Login to Azure management portal and click 'New' at the bottom left corner.

Step 2 – Select Network Services → Traffic Manager → Quick Create.

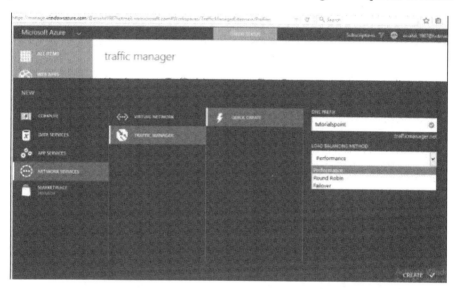

Step 3 – Enter the DNS prefix and select the Load Balancing Method.

There are three options in this dropdown.

- **Performance** – This option is ideal when you have endpoints in two different locations. When a DNS is requested, it is redirected to the region closest to the user.

- **Round Robin** – This option is ideal when you want to distribute the traffic among multiple endpoints. Traffic is distributed in round robin fashion by selecting a healthy endpoint.

- **Failover** – In this option, a primary access point is set up, but in case of failure alternate endpoints are made available as backup.

Step 4 – Based on your needs you can choose a load balancing method. Let's choose performance here.

Step 5 – Click create.

You will see the traffic manager created and displayed in your management portal. Its status will be inactive until it is configured.

Create Endpoints to be Monitored via Traffic Manager

Step 1 – Select the 'Traffic Manager' from the left panel in the management portal that you want to work on.

Step 2 – Select 'Endpoints' from the top horizontal menu as shown in the following image. Then select 'Add Endpoints'.

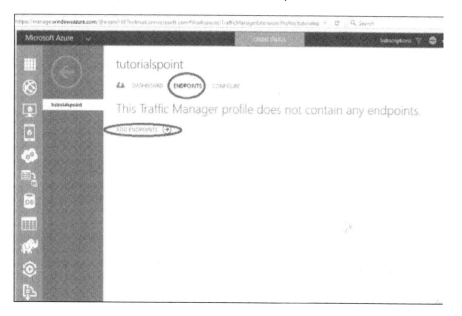

Step 3 – The screen shown in the following image will appear. Choose the service type and items under that service will be listed.

Step 4 – Select the service endpoints and proceed.

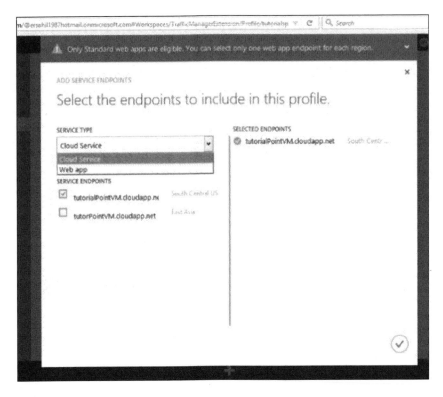

Step 5 – The service endpoints will be provisioned.

You can see that in this case, the service 'tutorialsPointVM' created in Azure will now be monitored by the traffic manager and its traffic will be redirected according to the specified policy.

Configure the Policy

Step 1 – Click on 'Configure' in the top menu bar as shown in the following image.

Step 2 – Enter the DNS Time to Live (TIL). It is the amount of time for which a client/user will continue to use a particular endpoint. For example, if you enter 40 seconds the traffic manager will be queried after every 40 seconds for the changes in the traffic management system.

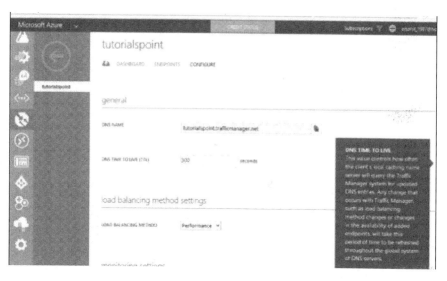

Step 3 – You can change the load balancing method here by choosing a desired method from the dropdown. Here, let's choose 'Performance' as chosen earlier.

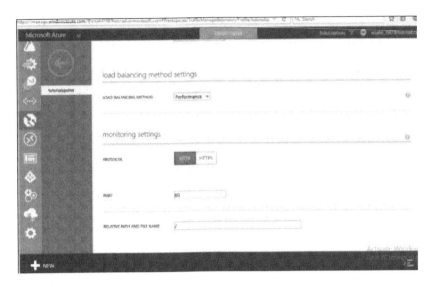

Step 4 – If you scroll down, you will see heading 'Monitoring Setting'. You can choose the protocol; enter port number and relative path for a service to be monitored.

Microsoft Azure - PowerShell

PowerShell is a framework or you can say an interface built by Azure team that lets the user to automate and manage Windows Azure services. It is a command line tool that uses the scripts or cmdlets to perform tasks such as creating and managing storage accounts or Virtual Machines that can easily be done using the preset commands.

Installing Azure PowerShell

Step 1 – Login into Azure Management Portal.

Step 2 – Click 'Downloads'.

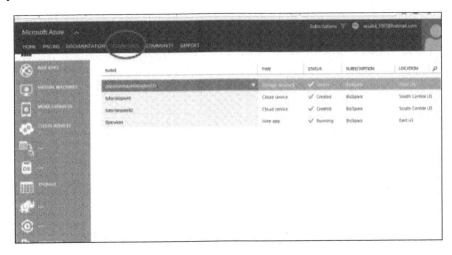

Step 3 – In the following screen, locate 'command-line tools' and then 'Windows Azure PowerShell'. Click 'Install' listed under it to download the setup and install it.

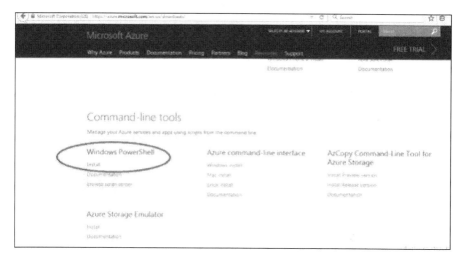

Alternatively, you can visit the link
http://www.windowsazure.com/en-us/manage/downloads/

Connecting to Your Subscription

Once you have installed Azure PowerShell, you will have to connect it to your Azure subscription.

Step 1 – Locate Microsoft 'Azure PowerShell' in your programs.

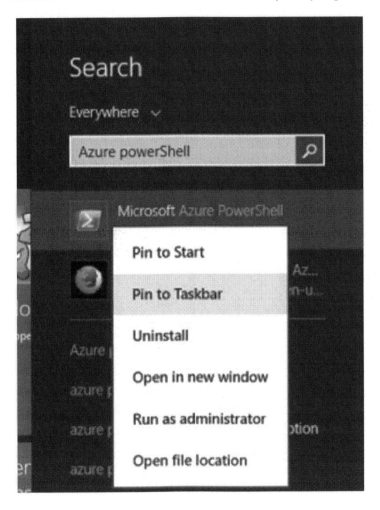

Step 2 – Pin it to the taskbar. You can run it as ISE by pinning it to the taskbar in Windows 8. Somehow, if it doesn't show the option of 'Run ISE as Administrator' it is in programs. ISE lets copy paste commands easily.

Step 3 – Right-click on 'Microsoft Azure PowerShell' and select 'Run ISE as Administrator'.

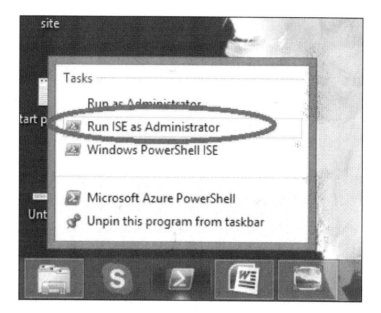

Connect to Your Azure Account
Using Active Directory

To get started with Azure tasks, you will have to first add your Azure account to PowerShell. You just have to perform this step once on your computer and every time you run Azure PowerShell, it will connect to the account automatically.

Step 1 – Enter the following cmdlet in PowerShell.

```
Add-AzureAccount
```

Step 2 – The screen shown in the following image will pop up and ask for credentials of your account. Enter the credentials and sign in.

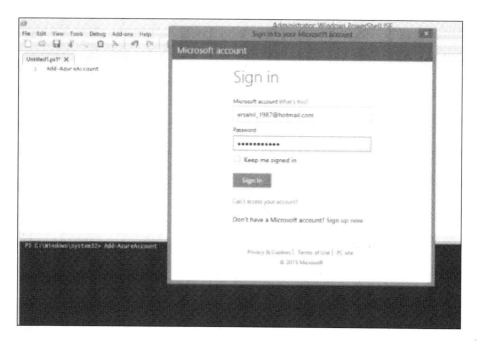

Step 3 – Now you are ready to perform tasks in Azure using Azure PowerShell.

Using Certificate

In this method, you can download a certificate on your machine and login to our account using that certificate.

Step 1 – Enter the following cmdlet in PowerShell. You will be prompted to save a file and the file will be downloaded on your computer with the extension. *publishsettings*.

```
Get-AzurePublishSettingsFile
```

You will see a similar file on your computer.

Step 2 — Enter the following cmdlet. Highlighted part is the path of the file downloaded in previous step. Also replace the name of the file with yours

```
Import-AzurePublishSettingsFile C:\Users\Sahil\Downloads\BizSpark-11-
  5-2015credentials.publishsettings
```

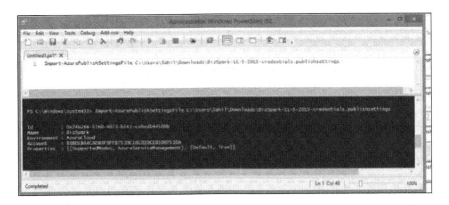

Step 3 — Just to make sure that everything has gone right. Run the following cmdlet. It will display the details of your account and subscription.

```
Get-AzureAccount
  Get-AzureSubscription
```

You can add many accounts to Azure PowerShell.

Remove Azure Account

Run the following cmdlets. Replace the highlighted part with your account ID. It will ask for your confirmation and it is done.

```
Remove-AzureAccount -Name myaccount@somesite.example
```

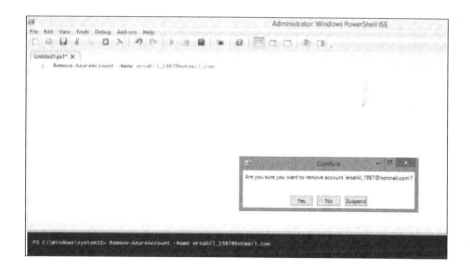

Get Help

The following cmdlet will list all the commands available for Azure tasks.

```
Get-Help Azure
```

There are lots of tasks that can be managed using PowerShell such as creating and managing web applications, storage accounts, virtual machines, etc. In fact, many users find it quicker and better as compared to Azure Management Portal. To manage the Azure Storage using PowerShell refer to Table, Blobs and Queues chapter in this tutorial.

Microsoft Azure - Monitoring Virtual Machines

Monitoring virtual machines is important to keep a track of its performance and health. Windows Azure provides an interactive interface to monitor the statistics related to the performance of virtual machine. The five key statistics are –

- CPU percentage
- Disk Read Bytes/sec
- Disk Write Bytes/sec
- Network in
- Network out

Monitor VM in Azure Management Portal.

Step 1 – Login to Azure Management Portal.

Step 2 – Go to Virtual Machine.

Step 3 – Select the virtual machine you want to monitor.

Step 4 – Select Monitor from the top menu as shown in following image.

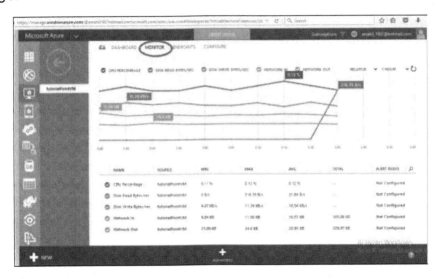

You can see 5 key terms on the above screen. It seems pretty complicated at first glance but when you look carefully, you can see that each line on the graph is in a different color which matches the color of the term. For example, CPU Percentage is in purple color and the purple line on the graph represents it. The machine shown in the above image is quite new. The following sections will explain how figures are read.

CPU Percentage

CPU percentage is the most common statistics to check whenever there is a performance issue in an application. It tells the processor's utilization in percentage. In the following image, you can see that in the last dropdown at the right top corner 1 hour is selected and, highest utilization is at 3:15 which is 0.13%.

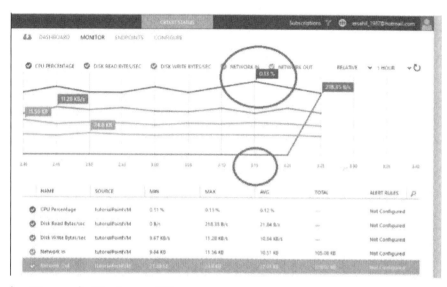

Disk Read Bytes/Sec

Another factor affecting performance is disk input/output operations. Disk read byte/second measures the amount of data read every second on the disk. If the read operations are done more frequently on the disk, performance issues can be resolved using a faster disk.

Disk Write Bytes/sec

Similarly, disk write byte/sec measures the amount of data written every second. If the application needs writing large amount of data on the disk, a bigger disk can be chosen.

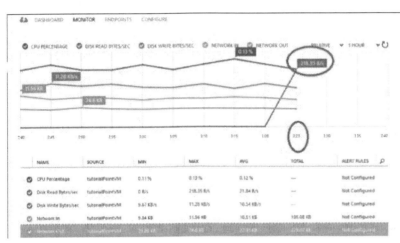

In the image above, you can see the highest point in disk read is 218.35 byte/sec at 3:25. You can see the last hour's data because '1 Hour' is selected in the dropdown. You can also see data for last 24 hours and 7 days.

Network In

Monitoring the network traffic can be done by looking at the 'network in' figures in the 'Monitor' section. The network-in statistics can be in bytes or TCP segments received.

Network Out

Network-out statics tells about TCP segments sent per second. You can also see relative or absolute statistics by selecting an option from dropdown encircled in the following image.

Similarly, you can choose the duration from the dropdown highlighted in the following image.

You can also choose particular metrics, by clicking on 'Add Metrics' at the bottom of the screen. The following screen will appear, in which you can check the desired metrics.

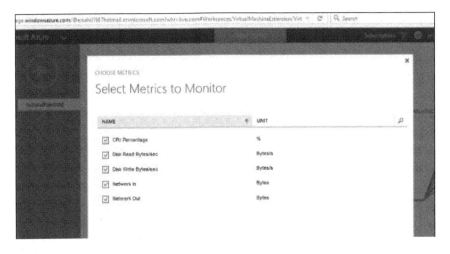

Enable Diagnostics

Enabling diagnostics allows you to collect logs. Azure will collect logs and store in a storage account you specified. We can enable diagnostics by switching to the 'Preview Portal'. Diagnostic figures help in troubleshooting as the logs for errors can be tracked in the storage account.

Step 1 – Switch to the 'preview portal'.

Step 2 – Locate the 'Virtual Machine (classic)' in the left panel.

Step 3 – Select the Machine and 'All Settings'.

Step 4 – Scroll down and locate 'Diagnostics'. Select 'Diagnostic' as shown in the following image.

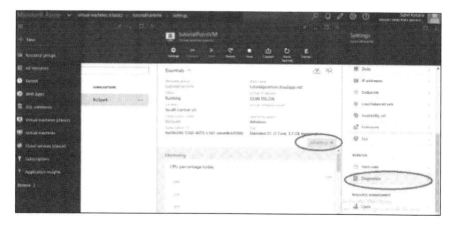

Step 5 – Select 'On' in the next panel displayed on the right side. By default it will be set off.

Step 6 – Since it uses a storage account to store the logs you will have to configure the setting for the storage account by clicking on the encircled part in the following image.

Step 7 – You can also select or deselect the type of logs you want to keep.

You will also see a panel at the bottom with the heading 'Monitoring'. This section displays the same metrics that we discussed in the section above.

These figures help users to identify the causes of performance slide of an application. They can also generate alerts for these features; they go above the set limits.

Microsoft Azure - Setting Up Alert Rules

While monitoring a virtual machine we can see different metrics related to a virtual machine in Azure. Azure has also provisioned a way to alert the administrator of virtual machine when these metrics go above or below a specified limit through e-mail. Setting up an alert can be very useful in notifying the administrator about issues that require attention.

Step 1 – Go to the 'Monitoring' section of your virtual machine.

Step 2 – Select the metrics you want to set alert for.

Step 3 – Select 'Add Rule' from the bottom.

Step 4 – Enter the name for alert and enter other information.

Step 5 — In the following screen that pops up, select condition. It can be greater than, less than or equal to.

Step 6 — Enter the threshold value which will be in percentage. In this example, let's enter 85 which means you will get an e-mail when utilization for processor of your virtual machine reaches the 85% average over the last 10 minutes.

In addition to sending the alert e-mail to service administrator and co-administrators, you can receive alert in one more e-mail.

You can set maximum 10 alerts for each subscription. Alerts can be sent to the administrator's e-mail plus one more e-mail provided at the time of setting up an alert.

Similarly, you can set alerts for other Azure services like web applications and mobile applications.

Microsoft Azure - Application Deployment

In this chapter, we will discuss different ways of deploying an application on Windows Azure. When we say application, it can be a web application or a mobile application. Earlier web apps were called websites, but now everywhere they are referred as web applications. We will be discussing how to deploy applications from Visual Studio and management portal in the chapter 'Websites'.

Deploying a Web App from PowerShell

To get started with the PowerShell, refer to 'PowerShell' chapter in the tutorial. In order to deploy a website from PowerShell you will need the deployment package. You can get this from your website developers or you if you are into web deployment you would know about creating a deployment package. In the following sections, first you will learn how to create a deployment package in Visual Studio and then using PowerShell cmdlets, you will deploy the package on Azure.

Create a Deployment Package

Step 1 – Go to your website in Visual Studio.

Step 2 – Right-click on the name of the application in the solution explorer. Select 'Publish'.

Step 3 – Create a new profile by selecting 'New Profile' from the dropdown. Enter the name of the profile. There might be different options in dropdown depending on if the websites are published before from the same computer.

Step 4 – On the next screen, choose 'Web Deploy Package' in Publish Method.

Step 5 – Choose a path to store the deployment package. Enter the name of site and click Next.

Step 6 – On the next screen, leave the defaults on and select 'publish'.

After it's done, inside the folder in your chosen location, you will find a zip file which is what you need during deployment.

Create a Website in Azure using PowerShell

Step 1 – Enter the following cmdlets to create a website. Replace the highlighted part. This command is going to create a website in free subscription. You can change the subscription after the website is created.

```
New-AzureWebsite -name "mydeploymentdemo" -location "East US"
```

If cmdlet is successful, you will see all the information as shown in the above image. You can see the URL of your website as in this example it is mydeploymentdemo.azurewebsites.net.

Step 2 – You can visit the URL to make sure everything has gone right.

Deploy Website using Deployment Package

Once the website is created in Azure, you just need to copy your website's code. Create the zip folder (deployment package) in your local computer.

Step 1 – Enter the following cmdlets to deploy your website.

```
Publish-AzureWebsiteProject -name "mydeploymentdemo" -package
    "C:\Users\Sahil\Desktop\deploymentDemo\MyWebsiteOnAzure.zip"
```

Here in above commandlet, the name of the website just created is given and the path of the zip file on the computer.

Step 2 – Go to your website's URL. You can see the website as shown in the following image.

Microsoft Azure - Backup & Recovery

Azure backup can be used to backing up on-premise data in cloud. Data is stored in an encrypted mode. The following sections provide a detailed illustration of how to do it using Azure. In this process, we will first create a backup vault where our data will be stored and then see how data can be backed up from our on-premise computer. The backup agent which is installed on the computer, first encrypts the data and then sends it over the network to the storage place in Azure. Your data is completely safe and secure.

Create Backup Vault

Step 1 – Login into your management portal.

Step 2 – At the bottom right corner, select New → Data Services → Recovery Services → Backup Vault → Quick Create.

Step 3 – Enter the name of vault and select the region. It will be created and displayed in your management portal.

Step 4 – Select the vault and click 'Download Vault Credentials' as shown in the following image.

Step 5 – It will save a credential file on your computer.

Step 6 – Now scroll down the same page in Azure and you will see three options under 'Download Agent'. Select a suitable option. Let's choose the third option in the list in this example.

Step 7 – Agent's setup will be saved on your computer. You will have to install it by following the wizard. There is nothing very specific in the installation process.

Step 8 – At the end of the installation, you will see a button at the bottom of pop-up window 'Proceed to Registration'. Click that button and the following screen will appear.

Step 9 – First step is vault identification. Browse the credentials file on your computer which was saved in the last step.

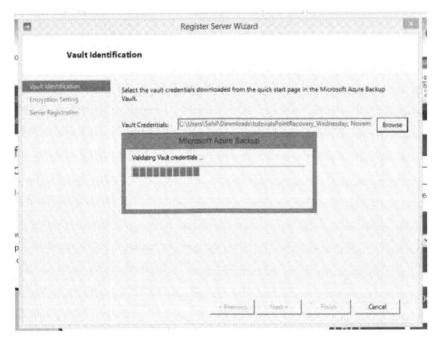

Step 10 – Next step in the registration wizard is choosing the encryption setting. You can enter your own passphrase or let the wizard generate it by itself. Here let's choose 'Generate Passphrase'.

Step 11 – Browse for the location where you want to save the passphrase. Keeping this passphrase file safe is very important as you won't be able to restore backups without it.

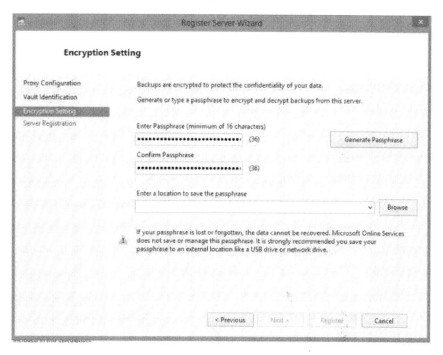

Step 12 – Click on Next and the file will be saved on your selected location.

Schedule a Backup

After the wizard in the above section is finished, you will see the following program that was installed in the previous step, running on your computer. You will come across selecting the data folder from your computer you want to back up on Azure and the frequency of backup in this wizard.

Step 1 – Click 'Schedule Backup' from the right panel.

In this example, let's select the data folder named 'QServicesManagementSystem'.

Follow the steps as pop up on the screen and are quite understandable. You are allowed to back up 3 times maximum and you can choose from daily and weekly frequency.

Step 2 – In the following step, select how long you want to keep the backup in your online storage. Set it according to your need.

Step 3 – You can choose the 'Backup Now' in the left panel of backup agent. It will save a copy of your data that very moment. Then you can see it in your management portal by selecting the backup vault and going to its dashboard.

You can see in the following image that there is one item listed under 'Jobs' section as data has been backed up by selecting 'backup now'. This section will display all the activities in backup task. Details of the backup schedule is displayed under 'Status' section.

Step 4 – You can recover the data by selecting 'Recover Data' in backup agent and following the wizard.

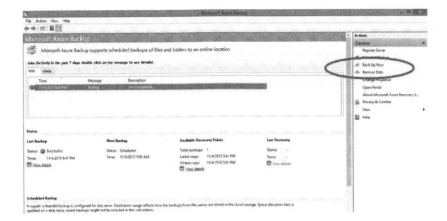

Microsoft Azure - Self-Service Capabilities

The self-service capabilities here refer to the ability to manage group, users profile and passwords. These capabilities are helpful in reducing the cost and labor of the IT departments. It enhances the user experience and removes the unnecessary hassle of asking for permissions of the administrator. Self-service capabilities enable the users to manage the mentioned services without compromising the security of the systems. Everything happens within the policies set by the organization.

Group Management

Let us say few people in an organization want to create one group where they can connect with each other for certain period of time. Usually, they will have to ask for the administrator to create a group for them. But in Azure active directory, one person can create a group and others can join the group without having to ask the administrator. Also, the group owner can handover the ownership of the group to someone else by himself.

Password Management

Azure Active directory offers the services that lets the users (client's employees or application users) to manage their password on their own. The end users can make a self- registration for password reset.

Additionally, this service includes the resetting and changing the password by the end users.

Self-service capability policies are completely controlled by the administrators of Azure Active directory. They can configure the policies in accordance with their organizations policy. They can view the reports on end user password resets, change, etc. This way administrators can monitor the user's activities for their account management, even after making them capable of self-service.

In order to use this service, organizations must subscribe to basic or premium version of Azure active directory. There is a detailed demonstration of self-service password reset and group management using Azure Active Directory in a separate chapter of this tutorial.

Microsoft Azure - Multi-Factor Authentication

All of us at some point have encountered multi-factor authentication. For example, customers of some banks receive a call or one-time password as text message on their mobile phones while signing in to their bank account online. The multi-factor authentication refers to the system in which more than one system authenticates the user to access an application. The multi-factor authentication offers better security for Azure clients. It lets the client choose if they want to use more than one system of credentials to allow the users to access the applications. Multi-factor authentication can be used to protect both on-premise and on-cloud directories.

In this process, the user first signs in with the username and password in a normal way. The credentials are verified and then if the automated call authentication is activated, the user receives a call and is asked to confirm the sign-in attempt.

- **Mobile App** – Mobile apps for all platforms (Android, iOS and Windows) are available. This app pushes a notification when a sign-in attempt is made and then the user can choose to authenticate, if it is genuine attempt.

- **Text Message** – This method sends a one-time password to the registered mobile phone of the user. They either reply from their phone or enter the one-time password into their sign-in page.

- **Automated Call** – The automated call asks for the user to validate the sign-in attempt by pressing a key on their phone's dial pad.

Create a Multi-Factor Authentication Provider

Step 1 – Click 'New' at the left bottom corner → App Services → Active Directory → Multi Factor Auth Provider → Quick Create.

Step 2 – Enter the name for the provider.

Step 3 – Select Usage model. Let's choose 'Per Authentication' for this example. Please note that you won't be able to change the usage model once multi-authentication provider is created. So please take your needs in consideration before choosing it.

Step 4 – Next, there is an option, if you wish to link the existing directory or not. Here, let's link an existing directory name 'tutorialspoint' that was previously created to this multi-factor provider.

Step 5 – After you click 'Create', it will be listed in your services list. Select the multi-factor provider you just created and you will the following screen.

Step 6 – Select 'Manage' at the bottom of the screen and you will be taken to a new page as shown in the following image.

Step 7 – Select 'Configure' to choose the authentication.

Step 8 — You can set the number of attempts, change the phone number from where the call is made (default number is already there), two-way message timeout (default is 60 seconds), one-time password's timeout (default is 300 seconds) under general settings. You can also provide an e-mail address where you can be notified if one-time password is bypassed.

Step 9 — Scroll down the page and you will see fraud settings. Under Fraud Setting, you can choose to allow the users to send fraud alerts, block the user if an alert is reported and also set an e-mail address where alerts are sent.

Fraud Alert

☑ Allow users to submit Fraud Alerts

    ☑ Block user when fraud is reported

    Code To Report Fraud During Initial Greeting

    [   ]

    Send fraud alert notifications to these email addresses

    sangeeta@qservicesit.com

Account Lockout (PIN Mode Only)

☑ Lock user account after [4] consecutive Multi-Factor Authentication denials

    ☑ Reset account lockout counter after [10] minutes

    ☑ Unlock account after [10] minutes

    Send account lockout notifications to these email addresses

    sangeeta@qservicesit.com

[Save]

After the multi-factor authentication is activated for the users, they will be asked to choose one of the three methods (automated message, text message or mobile app) when they sign in to their account next time. The chosen method will be used to authenticate them each time they sign in to their account.

Enable the Multi-Factor Authentication for Existing Directory

One way is to link the directory to multi-factor authentication provider while creating it, as we seen in the previous section. However, you can also do it in the following way for a particular user.

Step 1 – Go to your directory by choosing it from the left panel and click 'Manage MultiFactor Auth' at the bottom of the screen.

Step 2 – It will take you to the following screen. Here you can select the user and enable or disable the multi-factor authentication for the user.

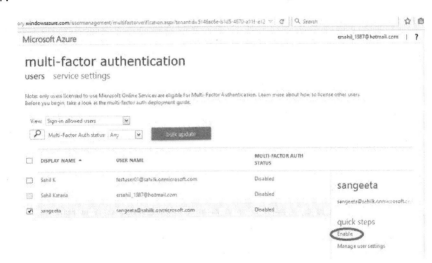

Enable Multi-Factor Authentication for On-premises Applications

When you create a new multi-authentication provider using the management portal and select to manage it, you are taken to the page as was shown in the first section of this chapter. If you want to enable the multi-factor authentication for your on-premise application, you have to install the authentication server by clicking the highlighted link. Then you can configure the setting as desired.

Step 1 – Click the link encircled in the following image.

Step 2 – You will be taken to the following screen, download the setup and generate activation credentials in order to login to the server.

Microsoft Azure - Forefront Identity Manager

Forefront Identity Manager (FIM) is an identity management software that manages the user's profiles on premises of the organization. It is also known as Microsoft Identity Manager (MIM) or Microsoft Forefront Identity Manager (MFIM). We discussed about Azure Active Directory in this tutorial earlier. FIM is an on-premise version of Azure Active Directory. This software was in existence long before Windows Azure services were launched. As the cloud services evolved, there was a need of user's profile management in Azure as well. Thus, Microsoft improved the software with the ability to link it with the Azure Active Directory.

Imagine a situation in which a company has their partial data or extended infrastructure on the cloud. This brings up the need of providing access to end user's on both the locations (on-premise and cloud). FIM lets the users access the data on cloud securely. It also handles the synchronization. It is a very easy interface to create users, set password, and authorize users to reset their own passwords.

Experts find FIM less complex and easy to operate as compared to other identity management software. Also it is easy to use synchronies and use in the environment where Microsoft products are being used.

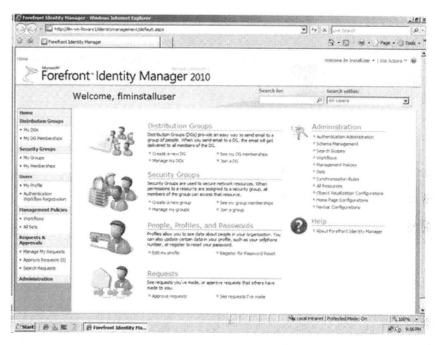

FIM can be connected to Azure Active Directory using the tool Forefront Identity Manager Connector for Windows Azure Active Directory. This tool helps to synchronize the data on-premise in FIM to the Azure Active Directory.

Once you have downloaded and installed the tool, you have to simply follow the wizard, in order to connect your FIM information with on-cloud Azure Active Directory.

Microsoft Azure - Data Import & Export Job

This is very useful service for the clients in case a large amount of data cannot be accessed over the network from their storage account. Azure gives an option to its clients that they can put their data on a hard drive and ship them to Azure datacenters. That data is then uploaded to their storage account. Similarly, if data is needed to be downloaded by the client that is not viable to do over the network, they can ship an empty hard drive to the datacenter and Azure team will copy the data to that drive and ship it back to the client. In both cases, the data is encrypted.

Data Export Job

Let's assume you have a large amount data in your Azure storage account and you want a copy of that data.

Create an Export Job

In this process, you will be given a shipping address, to where the empty hard drives needs to be shipped.

Step 1 – Login to Azure management portal and select the 'Storage' from the left panel.

Step 2 – Select the storage account.

Step 3 – Click 'Import/Export' from the top menu.

Step 4 – Create 'Export Job'.

The following screen will pop up.

Step 5 – On clicking the next arrow, you will see the following screen, where you will have to provide your contact and shipping details.

Step 6 – In the next screen, you will have to select the Blob Data you want to export. You can specify the path or choose to export all blob data from the storage account.

Step 7 – Enter a name for job in lower case letters. Address you can see here is the address where the hard drives is to be shipped. This address is based on the location of my storage account.

Step 8 – In the next step, you will have to provide the shipping details of the hard drive for delivery to datacenter and return to your location.

Step 9 – Click next and you are done.

Hard Drives to Be Shipped

In order to determine how many hard drives you need for the Blob data, you will have to use **Microsoft Azure Import/Export Tool**. You will have to download and install this tool on your machine. Only 3.5 inch SATA hard drive I/II are up to 6TB supported.

Ship the Hard Drives

You need to ship the hard drives to the shipping address obtained while creating the export job. Then you need to come back to the management portal to enter the tracking number, in case you chose to provide the tracking number after shipping in the screen above.

Decrypt the Data

You will have to enter the decryption key before reading the data on hard drives. You can get the decryption key from your management portal by selecting the job name.

Data Import Job

If you want to store the large amount of data to your storage account, you can do so by saving it on the hard drive and shipping it to the datacenter.

Prepare the Hard Drives

You will have to use **Microsoft Azure Import/Export Tool** to prepare the hard drives. As mentioned in earlier section, the only 3.5 inches SATA hard drives are supported for this purpose. This process will create a drive journal file that you will need while creating the import job in management portal. The journal file will be saved on your computer.

Create Import job

Step 1 – Login into the management portal and go to the storage account.

Step 2 – Select 'import/export' at the bottom of the screen.

Step 3 – Select 'Create Import Job'.

Step 4 – Check the checkbox and click Next.

Step 5 – In the next screen, provide the contact details of the return shipping address. Enter the details and click Next.

Step 6 – Upload the Drive Journal File that was created while preparing the hard drive.

Step 7 – Enter the name for import job.

Step 8 – Enter the shipping details for the delivery of hard drives to the datacenter and return to your location.

Ship the Hard Drives to the Datacenter

Ship the hard drive to the address obtained while creating import job in the management portal. Enter the shipping tracking number for the job in the management portal in order to complete the job.

Microsoft Azure - Websites

There is a detailed description of how to create websites in Azure in the chapter, 'Compute Module'. Azure websites service is named 'Web Apps' everywhere in the management portal so don't get confused. This chapter will discuss few more terms associated with Azure websites. In normal hosting environment, developers usually encounter problem when they deploy their websites in production. Azure websites service ensures that developers encounter least problems while deploying their websites. Also, Azure website service comes under PaaS (Platform as a Service). This means that websites can be deployed without actually having a full-fledged infrastructure.

Create a Website in Azure Management Portal

Just to reconnect with the website creation, let's take a look at these steps of how to create a website in Azure Management portal.

Step 1 – Login to your management portal.

Step 2 – Click 'New' at the left bottom corner of the screen → Compute → Web Apps → Quick Create.

Step 3 – Enter the details as shown in the picture above and click 'Create Web App'.

Step 4 – Go back to websites in your management portal and you will see it listed. Click the URL.

You will be taken to the website that you just created.

Deploying Azure Website from Visual Studio

Let's publish our website from Visual Studio in the domain name we just created. After a website or web application is created in Visual Studio.

Step 1 – Go to Solution Explorer and right click on the website/webapp name.

Step 2 – Choose 'publish'.

Step 3 – In this step, you need to connect to Azure subscription account in order. Click 'Import'.

Step 4 – Click 'Add Azure Subscription'.

Step 5 – For the first time, you will have to 'Download Subscription file'.

Step 6 – The above step will download a file with extension .publishsetting on your computer (if you are not logged in, it will ask you to login before downloading).

Step 7 – Come back to the same pop-up and now browse for the file that was just downloaded.

Step 8 – Now expand the dropdown and you will see the websites available in your subscription. As in the picture below you can see two websites. Let's select 'tutorialsPoint'.

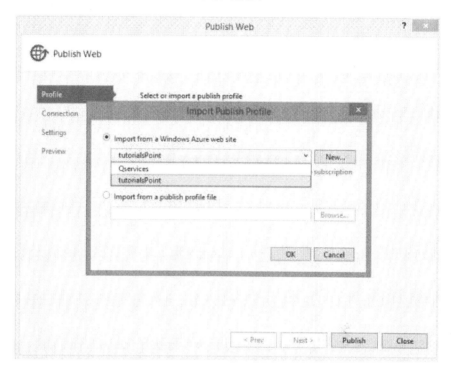

Step 9 – On the following screen, leave the defaults on. There are many options for public methods. We need 'Web Deploy' method here. Click 'Validate Connection'.

Step 10 – On the next screen, again the leave the defaults on.

Step 11 – Finally on the last screen, click publish.

Step 12 – Go to the URL of website and you will see your content.

You can see how easy it is to deploy a website in Azure using Visual Studio. You can make changes in Visual Studio and publish it from there itself. This makes testing of applications very easy.

Monitoring the Website

In the management portal, if you go to the website's dashboard you can see the figures related to the website. You can control lots of things related to your website from this section of your management portal. You can see the website metrics, create backup, configure setting, and scale the website.

Step 1 – To see the website metric, select monitor from top menu and you will see the following screen.

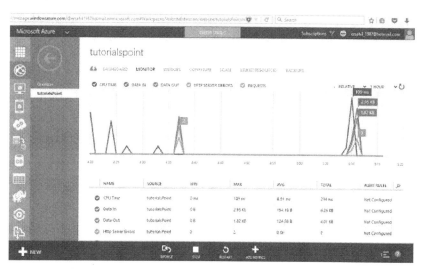

Step 2 – Go to the website and select 'Dashboard' from the top menu.

Step 3 – Scroll down and you will see the following information.

Staged Publishing

Windows Azure enables the deployment of a website in stages. You can create the deployment slots.

Add a Deployment Slot for Testing Before Production

Basically, this feature allows you to deploy your website in a separate slot for testing purpose and then switch the slot. If anything goes wrong, you can simply go back to the previous version by changing the slot. Sometimes, applications don't behave well as they are expected to at a large scale, this feature comes handy in such situations. This makes deployment tasks very easy for developers and organizations.

Microsoft Azure - Scalability

Scaling is adaptability of the system to the changed amount of workload or traffic to the web application. One of the great features of Azure service is its ability to auto scale according to the demands of the application usage.

Basically, increasing or decreasing the resources for application is called scaling. Instance is created each time a web app is deployed. Creating the instance means assigning a server to that application. Increasing the instance means adding up the servers assigned to that application. The scaling is done by creating more instances which is called **scaling out**. Another way of achieving the scaling is provisioning the larger role instances, also called **scaling up**.

Configuring scaling is easier in Azure as compared to traditional hosting. The primary server does not need to be taken down. It also eliminates the physical constraints of adding resources.

Scaling features depend on the app service plan you opt for in Azure. There are five App service plans in Azure –

	Maximum Instances	Auto-scaling Supported
F	1	No

S	1	No
B	3	No
S	10	Yes
P	50	Yes

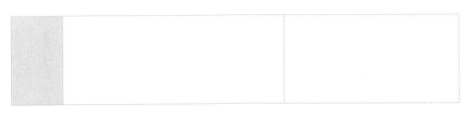

In free and shared service plan, you cannot scale the application as only one instance is available. In basic plan, you can scale the application manually. This means you have to check the metrics manually to see if more instances are needed and then can increase or decrease them from your Azure management portal. In standard and premium plan, you can choose to auto scale based on few parameters.

To see the all options available in different plans –

Step 1 – Go to your web app in the management portal and select 'scale' from the top menu. You can see under free service plan only 1 instance is created.

Step 2 – Under shared plan, you can create 1 instance but you don't have the option of auto scaling.

Step 3 – Under basic service plan, you can create up to 3 instances but do have option to auto scale. That means you can increase instances manually when you need to. Moreover, you can choose the size of the instance.

Step 4 – Under standard service plan, you can chose auto-scaling based on –

CPU percentage – You can choose to increase the instances depending upon the average CPU percentage over a specified period of time. In the following image, you can see we have chosen to increase the instances up to 3 if average CPU usage gets between 60% and 80%.

Schedule – You can set the number of instances that should run for a particular day of the week or for a particular time in a day.

Additionally, you can specify the dates when you need to increase the instances.

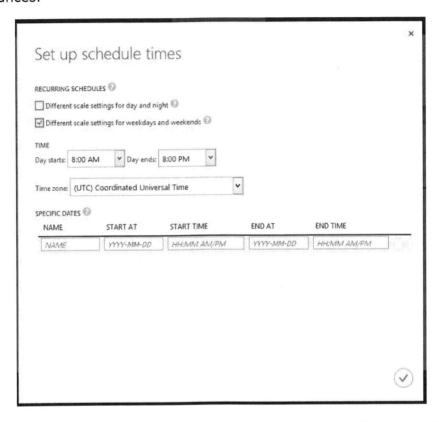

Here premium option for this application is not discussed. You might see different options based on your subscription for service plans. But the concept will remain the same.

Things to Consider

- You can change the service plan even after creating it.

- All the instances are from the same service plan. You cannot have one instance from shared and another from standard for the same application. Thus, you cannot mix and match instances from different service plans for the same application.

- Even if you have opted for auto-scaling, you should keep a check on metrics and performance of your application for the best out of Azure. This way you would be able to save money as well as optimize the performance of the applications.

Microsoft Azure - Disk Configuration

You would have noticed that we can attach a disk to a virtual machine that we create in Azure. We will be discussing those disks in this chapter. Disk here is referred to the data disks that can be stored on Azure. All kinds of disks are virtual hard drives with .vhd extensions. Vhds are the image file that stores the contents of physical hard drive. So they are images of the files, which we usually find on our computer's hard drive. There are two types of virtual hard disks –

- Operating system VHDs and Data Disks
- Image VHDs

On the basis of the extendibility, there are two types of VHDs –

- Fixed Size
- Dynamically Expanding

Azure supports only fixed sized VHDs. If you have to upload expandable VHD you will have to first convert it to fixed size VHDs. Maximum size supported by Azure is 1 terabyte for a disk.

Virtual Machine and Disks

When we create a virtual machine, it always resides in a storage account in Azure account. If there is no existing storage account in Azure, while attempting to create a virtual machine, Azure will automatically create one. If you already have a storage account, it will ask you to choose the storage account while creating a virtual machine. There is a detailed how-to on creating a virtual machine in this tutorial.

Create/Attach a Disk in Virtual Machine

Step 1 – Go to the virtual machine.

Step 2 – Select 'Dashboard' from the top menu.

Step 3 – Click 'Attach disk' → Attach empty disk at the bottom of the screen.

Step 4 – Enter the details in the following screen that pops up.

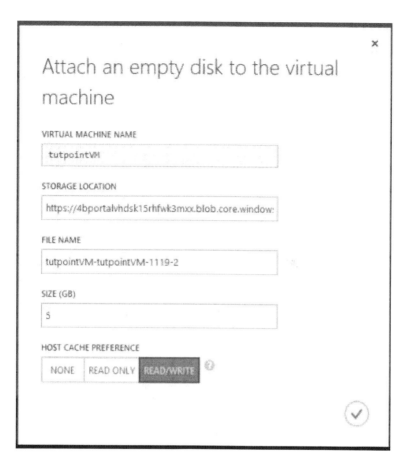

It will take few seconds to attach the disk to the virtual machine.

Configure the Disk in Virtual Machine

Step 1 – Connect to the virtual machine through .rpd file downloaded on your local machine.

Step 2 – In the virtual machine, right-click the windows icon at the left bottom corner and select 'Disk Management'.

Step 3 – You will see a message saying Disk is available on the screen. This is the same disk that you attached in the previous step.

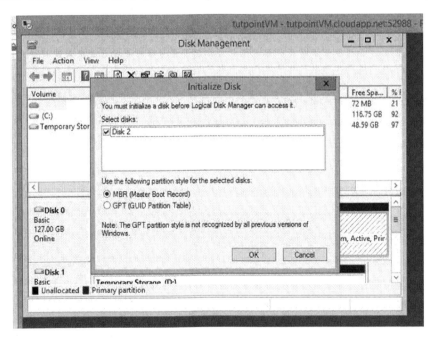

Step 4 – Before you can use it, you need to allocate it. You will see that it is still unallocated. Scroll down on the same screen and locate

the disk as shown in the following image, it is Disk 2. Right-click on it and select 'New Simple Volume'.

Step 5 – Follow the wizard. It will ask very general things, like naming the drive and file system. In the last screen, make sure to keep the quick format option checked.

Step 6 – After the wizard's job is over, you will be ready to use the disk. In this example, we have created the 'F' drive. You can create the folder and files or copy your data in the F drive.

Delete the Disk

You will have to first locate the disk in order to delete. Locating the right disk is very important. When you create a virtual machine you select the storage account for it. Disks reside in the storage account.

Step 1 – Go to the storage account of the virtual machine.

Step 2 – Click 'Containers' from the top menu.

Step 3 – Click vhd.

Step 4 – All the vhds in that storage account will be listed. This list will also contain the vhds from other virtual machines so be very careful while selecting the vhd.

Step 5 – Select the vhd you want to delete. You must know the name of the disk in order to identify it among the several vhds in the list (when you attach the disk you are prompted to enter the name of the disk).

Image Disks
Create an image from Virtual Machine

Step 1 – Go to the management portal.

Step 2 – Select the virtual machine you want to create an image of.

Step 3 – Click 'Dashboard' from the top menu.

Step 4 – Click the 'Capture' icon at the bottom of the window.

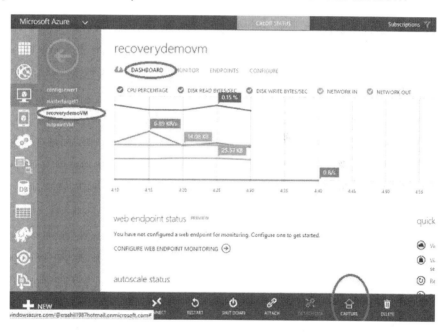

Step 5 – Name the image and enter the description.

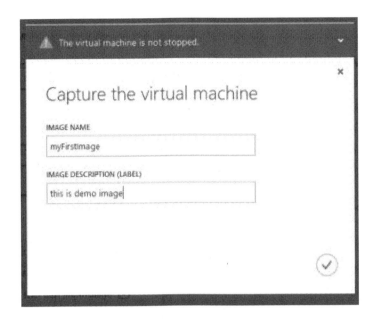

Step 6 – Once capturing is done, to find the image, follow the points given below –

- Select Virtual Machines from the panel. All the virtual machines in your account will be listed there.

- Click 'Images' from the top menu.

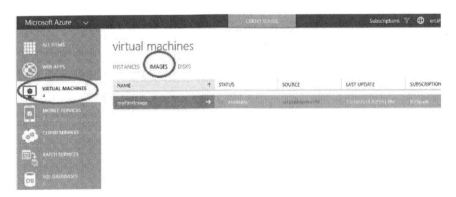

Create an Image from Your Computer

This is done through sysprep tool available in all modern Windows operating system.

Step 1 – Go C drive –> Windows –> System32 → Sysprep

Step 2 – Alternatively copy the following path in the address bar C:\Windows\System32\Sysprep

Step 3 – Run 'sysprep' application. This will create a VHD file on your computer which is the image of your machine.

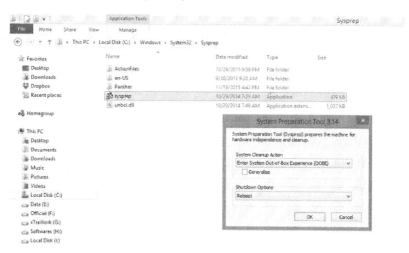

Considerations

You might get confused with the names of vhds, when you have multiple virtual machines under the same storage account. A way of knowing the name of the vhds associated with a particular machine is running 'Get-AzureDisk' cmdlet in Windows PowerShell. This cmdlet will get you all the details of disks in each virtual machine.

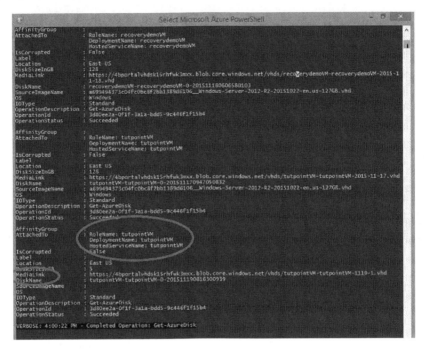

Step 1 – Run the following command

```
Get-AzureDisk
```

Step 2 – Locate your virtual machine name in the list. Under that virtual machine, check the diskname and medialink for your vhd name and link.

Microsoft Azure - Disk Caching

We saw in the previous chapter 'Disk Configuration', how we had to choose cache preference for the disk we attached. By default it is 'none'. We can choose read-only or read/write as per our requirements. This chapter will discuss how this setting affects the performance of input/output operations.

Attach an empty disk to the virtual machine ✕

VIRTUAL MACHINE NAME

recoverydemoVM

STORAGE LOCATION

https://4bportalvhdsk15rhfwk3mxx.blob.cor

FILE NAME

recoverydemoVM-recoverydemoVM-1119-

SIZE (GB)

HOST CACHE PREFERENCE

| NONE | READ ONLY | READ/WRITE | ?

HOST CACHE PREFERENCE
The host caching settings for an operating system disk or for a data disk improves performance under some circumstances. Host caching is off by default for both read and write operations for data disks. Host-caching is on by default for both read and write operations for operating system disks.

Normally, cache settings make considerable improvement when read-write operations with large amount of data are done. However, if lot of random I/O operations are done, turning the cache off is preferable as operations on cache incur charges on the basis of number of transactions. Random operations will not make any signification improvement in performance.

Read cache improves the performance, when data is read before, during input-output operations, and stored into cache. Also cache should be big enough to store all the data.

For all the OS disks, in-memory caching is done by default unless it is turned off manually by the user. If lots of random I/O operations on files are done in OS disks, it is better to move them in a data disk where by default cache is turned off. Cache settings can be manipulated using PowerShell command lets, APIs and Azure management portal. We can set the cache from the management portal while creating virtual machines and data disks.

Microsoft Azure - Personalize Access

We have two portals to access and manage our Azure service by logging in to our Azure account. Azure management portal has some issues with responsiveness, thus a second portal named preview portal was designed. The preview portal was launched later to improve the user experience on tablets and mobile devices.

Clients, who are managing their services through Azure portal, often come here and Azure team has provisioned the personalization of the look of Azure preview portal. Users can choose the color and features to be displayed on the dashboard, which makes it easy for them to navigate through the services in the portal. Let us see what can be personalized in Azure preview portal.

You can directly login to the preview portal by visiting https://portal.azure.com/ and using your Azure account or you can switch to it from Azure management portal. Azure team keeps making little changes but the overall concept remains the same. So when you try to customize your portal, it might look a little different but the basic features will remain the same.

Step 1 – Login to Azure management portal.

Step 2 – Switch to Azure preview portal by clicking on your photo and choosing 'Switch to Azure Preview Portal'.

Step 3 – You will see the following screen which is the dashboard of your Azure account. The tiles in the middle of the screen are some of the common tasks performed by Azure preview portal. To personalize these tiles click the 'Settings Icon' encircled.

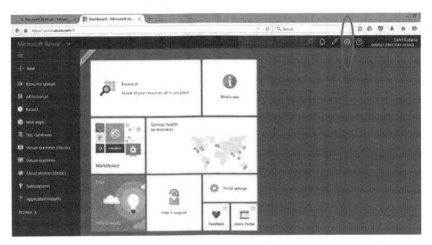

Step 4 – It will take you to the following screen. You can maximize the screen by clicking on the button encircled. You can choose from the available themes which will change the background color of the

screen. On the same screen, you can choose to show/hide the command labels that display the name of the command. Similarly, you can enable/disable the animations.

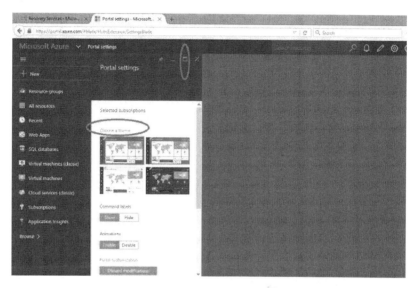

Step 5 — If you scroll down, you will see an option to change the language.

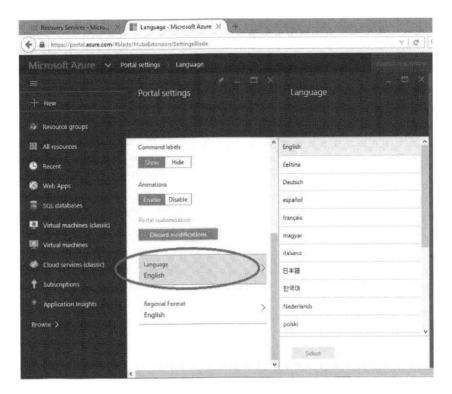

Step 6 – You can also change the size of the tile. You can make it bigger or smaller. For example, on the following screen if you want my resource groups bigger –

Right-click on the tile and choose customize.

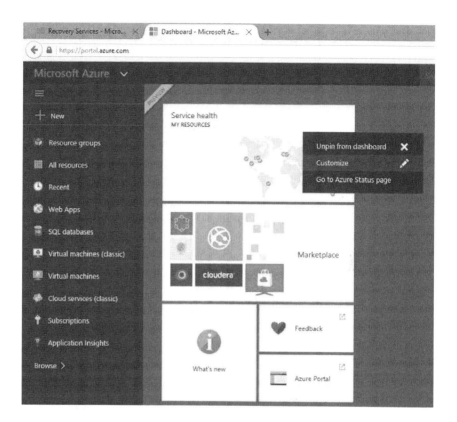

Alternatively, choose 'customize' from the top strip of the tile. It will appear when you hoover your cursor over it.

Choose the size of the tile. Click 'Done' on the top of the screen.

Step 7 – You can also customize your dashboard by moving the tiles as per your choice. You just have to drag and drop the tile to a different location on the screen.

Step 8 – You can pin any of your resources to the dashboard.

Go to the resource. Right-click on it or click the three dots.

Click on the 'Pin to Dashboard'.

When you come back to the dashboard by clicking on the 'Microsoft Azure' at the top left corner, you will see the resource there as shown in following image.

Azure - Personalize Company Branding

When a company has many applications, they might want to have the company's look and feel on the sign-in page of those applications. There could be several objectives behind this, including marketing. Companies that use Azure Active Directory for identity management can do it by customizing the appearance of the sign-in page.

This feature is available for basic and premium editions of Azure Active Directory. You won't find this in free edition.

If you don't have subscription to basic or premium edition you can have a free trial of premium edition.

Active Free Trial of Azure Active Directory (ADD) Premium Edition

Step 1 – Login to your Azure Management Portal.

Step 2 – Go to Azure Active Directory you want to work with.

Step 3 – Click on 'Licenses' tab from the top menu as shown in the following image.

Step 4 – Click 'Try Azure Active Directory Premium Now' and it will be activated for that directory.

Refresh your page as it might take a few seconds to update and show up on your portal. Once it is activated, you will see the plan under 'Licenses' tab.

Customize Branding

Before moving ahead, make sure that the images (logo, background, square background) you want to display on the sign-in page are of correct sizes and dimensions. If you don't take care of this, you would waste your time uploading images and then ultimately you will find that branding changes are not done. Here are certain specifications –

Image	Size in kb	Recommended Dimensions	Maximum Dimensions	Supported Format
Logo	5-10	60-280	60-300	Png jpeg
Square Logo	5-10	240-240	240-240	Png jpeg
Square Logo Dark Theme	5-10	240-240	240-240	Png jpeg
Sign-in page illustration	500 (300)	1420-1200	1420-1200	Png Jpeg gif

Step 1 – Go to the directory you want to work with.

Step 2 – Click on 'Configure' tab from the top menu.

Step 3 – Click 'Customize Branding' button. The following pop-up will appear.

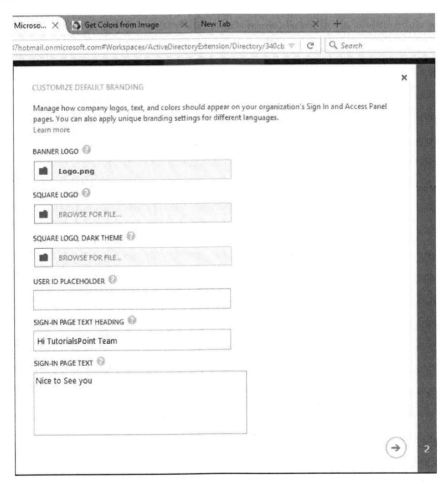

Step 4 – Enter the details and upload the images.

Step 5 – Click Next and enter the details.

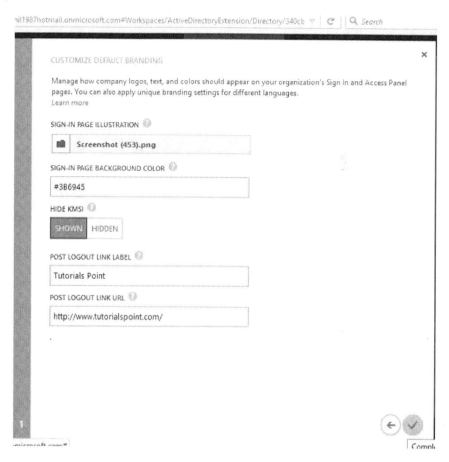

After you are done, do look for the notifications at the bottom of the window to make sure that changes are accepted. In the following image, you can see a notification in red outline which shows that it wasn't successful in a previous attempt and threw an error. If the changes are not accepted and an error occurs, click 'Details' button to find the cause. Usually this occurs when the size and dimension of images to be uploaded are not correct.

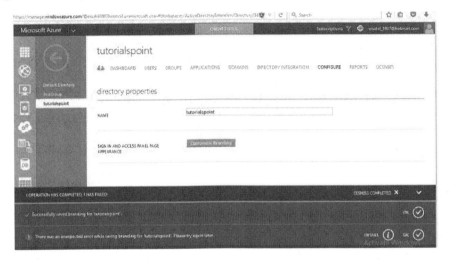

Login with Customized Sign-in Page

When you sign in to your organization's application, you will see your logo, big illustration image and sign-in text on that page. For example, let's sign in to Office 365 using organization's account.

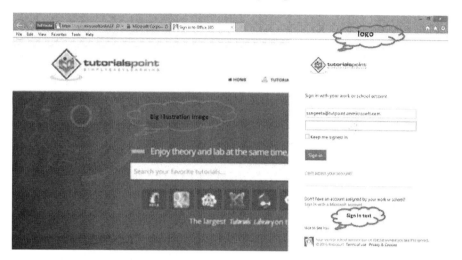

Things to Consider

- Domain name should be active.

- It might take up to an hour for changes to appear on the sign-in page.

- To test, choose 'in-private' session of internet explorer (or corresponding session in other browser where cookies don't affect your browsing).

Azure - Self-Service Password Reset

Users in your directory can be granted permission to reset their password, if they forget their password, in a few steps rather than having to ask the administrator to do so for them. This saves time and cost of the IT department or helpdesk dealing with such kind of tasks in an organization. Administrator can set the policy of resetting the password. This service is available in basic and premium edition of Azure Active Directory. In the chapter 'Personalize Company Branding' a small 'how-to' on getting a free trial of Azure Active Directory premium edition is included.

Step 1 – Login to the management portal.

Step 2 – Go to the active directory.

Step 3 – Click on the 'Configuration' tab.

Step 4 – Scroll down and locate 'User Password Reset Policy' heading.

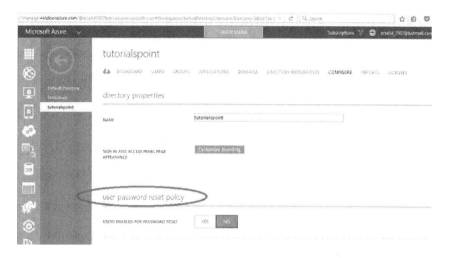

Step 5 – Click 'Yes' to enable users for password reset as shown in the following picture and scroll down to set the policy.

Step 6 – You can choose to allow users to reset their password in certain groups.

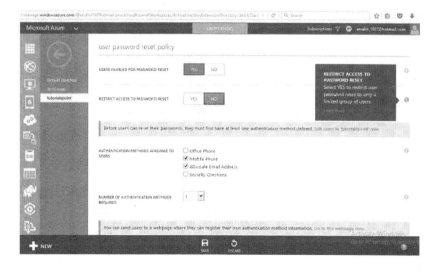

Step 7 – Refer to the image above; you have four options to choose from to authenticate the password reset. For example, let's choose two of them here. Users in this case will be able to use their mobile phone or alternate e-mail address to verify the password reset.

Step 8 – In 'Number of Authentication Methods Required' dropdown, if you choose 2 than users will have to provide two identification information (e.g. mobile phone and office phone). In this example, let's leave it as one.

Step 9 – Next option is whether you want them to register for self-password reset or not. If you choose 'No', the administrator will have to do it for each user individually.

Step 10 – 'Customize "Contact Your Administrator" link. You can give a specific webpage link or an e-mail id where the user can contact when he encounters a problem while resetting his password.

Step 11 – Click 'Save' at the bottom of the screen.

Next time when users login to access their account, they will be asked to register for password reset service where they can feed in their phone number or e-mail address. This information will be used when they forget/lose their password. In this example, as the policy set, they can choose from one of the options for verification code, through a call on their mobile phone, a text on their mobile phone or through an e-mail to an alternate email address.

Azure - Self-Service Group Management

Users can themselves create groups in the access panel. Let us see how to enable users to create and join groups.

Policy Setup for Self-service Group Management

Step 1 – Login into the management portal.

Step 2 – Go to the Active Directory.

Step 3 – Click 'Configure' tab from the top menu.

Step 4 – Scroll down and locate 'group management' heading. Here you can choose to let users create and manage their own group. There are 6 things that you need to set under this heading. Azure team keeps adding the features.

Step 5 – First option is 'Delegated Group Management enabled'. If you choose yes, it will allow you to handover authority to manage the groups to users through the access panel which is the main purpose.

Step 6 – Second option is whether users can create security groups.

Step 7 – Third option is you can choose either to allow all users to manage groups or some of them. If you choose 'Some' you will have to specify the group.

Step 8 – Fourth option is, it lets you enable/disable the users to create groups in Office 365.

Step 9 – Fifth option is, if you want to allow some of the users to create and manage groups for Office 365, you will have to specify them.

Step 10 – Last option, is to enable dedicated group. If you choose to enable them you will be asked to add the group members.

After you have made changes, a 'Save' button will appear at the bottom of the screen to save changes.

Microsoft Azure - Create a Group

In this section, we are creating a group. The user who creates the group is the owner of the group and he can add or delete members in the group. Since we granted permissions to users to create their own group in the previous step, any user in this directory can create and manage a group.

Step 1 – Go to the Access Panel by visiting myapps.microsoft.com

Step 2 – Login to your azure Account.

Step 3 – At the top, you will see 'Groups'. Click on it to create a new group.

Step 4 – Choose 'My groups/All' from the dropdown at the top.

Step 5 – Click on 'Create new Group'.

Step 6 – The following screen will pop up. Enter the name and description of the group.

Step 7 – You can let all users to join the group or choose them to ask for the group owner's approval before joining the group. I have chosen the first option in which approval of the owner is required. This means users who want to join the group other than users added, will have to ask for approval.

Step 8 – Choose the desired option and click 'Create'.

Step 9 – Come back to the 'Groups' page. To add members to the group, select the group. In this case, let's select 'Developers Group'.

Step 10 – Click 'Add Members'.

Step 11 – The following pop-up will list all the users in the directory. You can add the members by clicking on their name.

Step 12 – You can add/delete member, edit group's description, and delete group on this page. Also you can make someone else the owner of this group.

If someone wants to join the group, he will ask for the owner's approval. The owner will get a notification and will see the request in 'approvals' tab of the access panel as shown in the image above. Also, if someone has requested to join a group that is owned by someone else, he will see his requests here.

Microsoft Azure - Security Reports & Alerts

Azure Active Directory enables the administrator to view the security reports that contain different types of data.

Anomalies Reports

This contains any data of sign-in attempt which is normal. If the system detects anything abnormal during the sign-in, it is collected in anomalies report. There are 9 types of reports available under this category, as you can see in the following image.

To view these reports –

Step 1 – Login to the management portal and go to the active directory.

Step 2 – Click 'Reports' tab from the top menu.

Step 3 – Click on one of the categories you want to see data for under 'Anomalous Activity'.

Activity Reports

On the same screen, if you scroll down you will see few reports under the heading 'Activity Report'. These are the activities like password reset, registration, etc. Each report name is self-explanatory. Currently, there are 4 types of reports under this category.

If you click on one of them, you will be shown the details as in the following image. Here, let's look for the audit report. You can see 1 activity has come up. All other kinds of reports are listed in the left panel where you can easily navigate through them. Also, you can download the report in CSV format by clicking on the 'Download' button at the bottom of the screen.

Integrated Application

This category contains the reports of the usage of cloud application in the organization. This category provides an interactive way to monitor the applications usage.

For example, in the following screen when you click on 'Application Usage' in the left panel, you can see that there are 12 sign-ins in App Access Panel and 3 in Visual Studio application.

Search Activity of a Particular User

Azure Active Directory provides one more useful feature that allows the administrator to search an activity for a particular user. As soon as you click on the 'Reports' in the top menu, you will see the following screen. You just have to enter the user display name or the user principal name. You will see all directory activities.

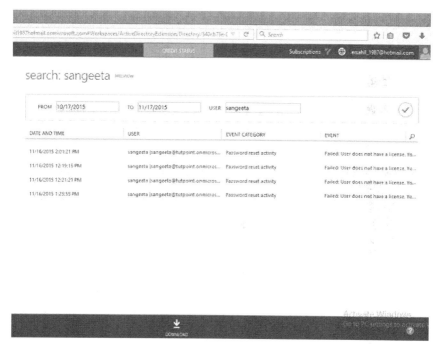

In the above screen, we have searched by entering the display name of the user and the user's activity details with time and date are listed on the screen.

Azure Active Directory Editions and Reports

All kinds of reports are not available in all the editions of Azure Active Directory. The following table lists the types of reports available in three editions of Azure Active Directory.

Report editions

REPORT	FREE	BASIC	PREMIUM
Anomalous activity reports			
Sign ins from unknown sources	✓	✓	✓
Sign ins after multiple failures	✓	✓	✓
Sign ins from multiple geographies	✓	✓	✓
Sign ins from IP addresses with suspicious activity			✓
Sign ins from possibly infected devices			✓
Irregular sign in activity			✓
Users with anomalous sign in activity			✓
Users with leaked credentials			✓
Activity logs			
Audit report	✓	✓	✓
Password reset activity			✓
Password reset registration activity			✓
Self service groups activity			✓
Integrated applications			
Application usage			✓
Account provisioning activity	✓	✓	✓
Password rollover status			✓
Account provisioning errors	✓	✓	✓
Rights managment			
RMS usage			RMS Only
Most active RMS users			RMS Only
RMS device usage			RMS Only

Microsoft Azure - Orchestrated Recovery

Orchestrated recovery is one of the features in Azure Site Recovery service. Azure Site Recovery automates the recovery of applications in case of failover at the primary site. This recovery is done in a coordinated way to restore the applications even if they have multi-tier workload. With multitier applications a coordinated recovery is essential to restore the service quickly, which is a challenging part of IT disaster and recovery tasks. However with the cloud technology, this has become very a simple and easy task.

In order to activate orchestrated site recovery you have to create a recovery plan. This can be done in Azure Management portal. The plans created for disaster recovery can be tested without interrupting the service.

Create a Site Recovery Vault

Step 1 − Login to your Azure management portal.

Step 2 − Click 'New' at the left bottom corner.

Step 3 − Click Data Services → Recovery Services −> Site Recovery Vault → Quick Create.

Step 4 − Enter the name and select the region. Make sure this vault is in the same region where virtual machines and networks are residing.

Step 5 − You will be redirected to the following screen. On the following screen, you can see a dropdown. If you expand the dropdown, you will see the different scenarios in which recovery can be configured.

Here you have to choose the recovery scenario according to the organization's requirements. Let's discuss each scenario in detail −

Between On-premises VMM Site and Azure

In this scenario, on-premises virtual machines are replicated to Azure. There are few prerequisite for this on-premise resources.

- Virtual machine server running on Windows server 2012 R2.

- Virtual machine server should have at least one cloud to be protected.

- Cloud should have at least one VMM host group and Hyper-V host server, or cluster and virtual machine on Hyper-V host server.

Setting up site recovery is a very methodological task. If you are not ready with all the prerequisites mentioned above, after going through few steps in the task you might have to revert back.

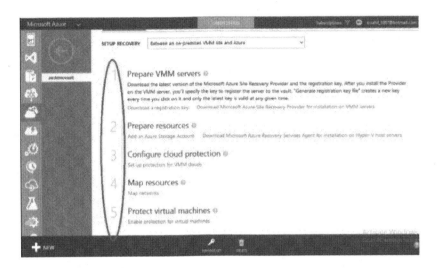

When you select this scenario from the dropdown you have to follow the five steps encircled in the picture above.

Between On-premises Hyper-V Site and Azure

This option is chosen for the replication of virtual machines residing on-premises Hyper-V server. The choice is suitable when Hyper-V server is running but VMM is not available.

Prerequisites (on-premises)

- On-site host should be Windows server 2012 R2 with Hyper-V role.

- Hyper-V should have at least one virtual machine.

Between On-premises Site with VMWare / Physical Server and Azure

This scenario replicates the physical servers to Azure. Also you have to choose this option from the dropdown when you need to replicate the VMware virtual machines residing at your premises. Protection is done in various ways like data is replicated over the internet. Before you begin the deployment, you must know the following terms. You will be configuring following servers while setting up site recovery in this scenario –

- **Process Server** – The data of the protected items is first sent to the process server where it is cached, compressed and encrypted. Then data is sent to the master target server.

- **Configuration Server** – This server is a communication link between protected items, process and master target server.

- **Master Target Server** – The master target server stores the data that is replicated from protected items.

PROJECT

1 Prepare Target(Azure) Resources ⊚

After you deploy the Configuration Server, download and copy the registration key file to the Configuration Server. Launch the installer on the Configuration Server and use the key file to register the server to the vault. Generate registration key file creates a new key every time you click on it and only the latest key is valid at any given time. After the Configuration Server has been registered, deploy the Master Target Server. Once deployed, log in into the server and register it to the Configuration Server.

Deploy Configuration Server   Download a registration key

Deploy Master Target Server   Download and install additional software (only for Linux Master Target Server)

2 Prepare Process Servers ⊚

After deploying Process Server, register them with the Configuration Server.

Download and install Process Server   Learn how to deploy Process Server

3 Add VMware vCenter Servers ⊚

Add VMware vCenter Servers

4 Protect Machines ⊚

Create Protection Group   Add Machines in Protection Group

MANAGE KEY   DELETE

Between Two On-premises VMWare Sites

Between Two On-premises VMM Sites and SAN Array Application

In this scenario, the on-premises VMM site is replicated to another site. The Hyper-V virtual machines on this site are protected through Storage Array Based (SAN) replication. An organization can take benefit from this option if it has an existing SAN infrastructure.

Prerequisites

The following image describes the prerequisite for this scenario to be deployed.

VMM prerequisites

- You'll need at least one VMM server in each on-premises site, deployed as a physical or virtual standalone server, or as a virtual cluster, running on System Center 2012 R2 with VMM update rollup 5.0.
- You should have at least one cloud on the primary VMM server you want to protect, and one on the secondary VMM server. The primary cloud you want to protect must contain the following:
  - One or more VMM host groups.
  - One or more Hyper-V clusters in each host group.
  - One or more virtual machines located on the source Hyper-V server in the cloud.

Hyper-V requirements

- You'll need a Hyper-V host cluster deployed in the primary and secondary sites, running at least Windows Server 2012 with the latest updates.

SAN prerequisites

- Using SAN replication you can replicate guest clustered virtual machines with iSCSI or fibre channel storage, or using shared virtual hard disks (vhdx). SAN prerequisites are as follows:
  - You'll need two SAN arrays set up, one in the primary site and one in the secondary.
- Network infrastructure should be set up between the arrays. Peering and replication should be configured. Replication licenses should be set up in accordance with the storage array requirements.
- Networking should be set up between the Hyper-V host servers and the storage array so that hosts can communicate with storage LUNs using iSCSI or Fibre Channel.
- See a list of supported storage arrays.
- SMI-S Providers, provided by the storage array manufacturers should be installed and the SAN arrays should be managed by the Provider. Set up the Provider in accordance with their documentation.
- Ensure that the SMI-S provider for the array is on a server that the VMM server can access over the network by IP address or FQDN.
- Each SAN array should have one or more storage pools available to use in this deployment. The VMM server at the primary site will need to manage the primary array and the secondary VMM server will manage the secondary array.
- The VMM server at the primary site should manage the primary array and the secondary VMM server should manage the secondary array.

Network prerequisites

You can optionally configure network mapping to ensure that replica virtual machines are optimally placed on Hyper-V host servers after failover, and that they can connect to appropriate VM networks. Note that:

- When network mapping is enabled, a virtual machine at the primary location will be connected to a network and its replica at the target location will be connected to its mapped network.
- If you don't configure network mapping virtual machines won't be connected to VM networks after failover.
- VM networks must be set up in VMM. For details read Configuring VM Networks and Gateways in VMM.
- Virtual machines on the source VMM server should be connected to a VM network. The source VM network should be linked to a logical network that is associated with the cloud.

Create a Recovery Plan

When you are done setting up site recovery for one of your chosen scenario, in your management portal you will have to create a recovery plan to orchestrate your recovery.

Step 1 — In the management portal, go to Azure Site Recovery vault you are working with.

Step 2 — Select 'Recovery Plans' from the top menu. You will see different options based on your choice of scenario and resources registered in the recovery vault.

Step 3 — You can create the recovery plan for site recovery as desired. It will also tell you any prerequisite task, in case you have missed any step in the process.

Step 4 — The customized plan created here can be executed in case of failover to orchestrate recovery. The services can be made available at a secondary site.

Microsoft Azure - Health Monitoring

Continuous health monitoring is one of the features of Azure Site Recovery. You don't have to subscribe to this feature exclusively. In the previous chapter, we saw how Azure Site Recovery can be configured for different scenarios. Once all the configurations are done, the Hyper-V recovery manager monitors the health of the protected resource instances continuously. It is done by Hyper-V recovery manager remotely from Azure. This procedure consists of collecting the metadata of virtual machines which is used for recovery.

What is happening in Azure Site Recovery is, the metadata is continuously collected for recovery purpose. Every time when data is transferred as a function of continuous health monitoring, it is always encrypted, thus it is safe and secure.

The data is replicated at the secondary site. The secondary site is made available in case of failover. In order to ensure that everything is working fine, test failover can be carried out. Planned and unplanned failovers are two circumstances in which the secondary site is to be made available. The planned failover is usually done for testing, maintenance, etc. while unplanned failover happens when a disaster occurs. No matter what kind of failover, the virtual machines on the primary site are continuously monitored and the metadata is collected. Thus, continuous health monitoring is a feature that keeps the data at the secondary site always available.

In addition to the back-up and orchestrated recovery, Azure Site Recovery continuously monitors the health of all its resource instances.

Microsoft Azure - Upgrades

Let us say, that our services are running fine on Azure. After sometime, we need to make changes and upgrade the services which are already running. Here comes the tricky part, sometimes upgrading would go smooth and sometimes you won't know what is causing the problem. Windows Azure has tried to address these issues.

Update a Cloud Service

The application code can be updated easily in Azure management portal. You will need a service package (.cspkg) and service configuration files (.cscfg) before moving ahead.

Step 1 – Login to the management portal.

Step 2 – Go to the service you want to update.

Step 3 – Click 'Instances' from the top menu and then click 'update'. The following screen will pop up.

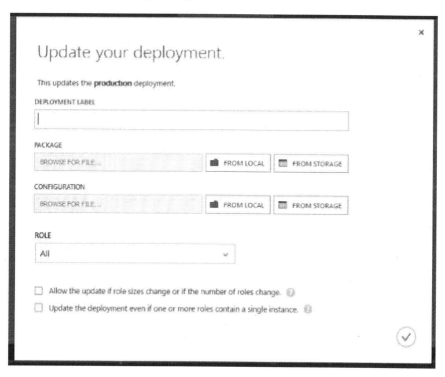

Step 4 – Enter the deployment label name and upload .cspkg and .cscfg files.

Step 5 – Select the role you want to update or select 'all' if want to update all roles.

Step 6 – Check the checkbox as required and click the 'Arrow' on the right side.

VIP (Virtual IP) Swap

You might come across a scenario, when you need to make changes to the architecture of service. Azure provisions a way which can handle the upgrading easily. There are two deployment environments - production and staging. Let's assume that your service is at production, but you can deploy the new version in the staging environment. After that you just test it and if everything is fine, you swap it with the production deployment. Behind the scene, the virtual IPs of production and staging deployment are swapped, hence staging becomes production and production becomes staging. While the swapping happens, the service is not interrupted. All this is done with no downtime for service. It also makes it easy to rollback to older production version in case you need to do it.

Step 1 – Login to the management portal.

Step 2 – Go to the service. Select 'Instances' from the top menu. You can see in the following screen, two instances are there for this service.

Step 3 – When you have deployed the service in staging and production you will see that 'Swap' at that bottom of the screen is activated. You just have to click that Swap icon and it will be done.

Considerations

- You can't swap if you have different number of endpoints for each deployment.

- It does not change the IP address of your service.

86274215R00170

Made in the USA
Middletown, DE
29 August 2018